Rag Dolls

Averina Hontoir

The Art of Crafts

First published in 2000 by
The Crowood Press Ltd
Ramsbury, Marlborough
Wiltshire SN8 2HR

British Library Cataloguing-in-Publication Data

A catalogue record for this book is available from the British Library.

ISBN 1 86126 247 7

Photographs and line artwork by Anthony Hontoir.

Typeset and designed by D & N Publishing
Baydon, Marlborough, Wiltshire.

Printed and bound by Leo Paper Products, China.

Contents

Introduction

Rag dolls have been made in one form or another for centuries. Before they began to be manufactured commercially in the middle of the nineteenth century, many of the dolls were treasured toys which mothers had made for their own children out of materials found around the house. If a mother could sew, there was no reason for her child not to have a toy. Rag dolls are still very popular today, and with the choice of materials now available, so many designs are possible, and children of all ages find the dolls soft to cuddle.

When you look at dolls that other people have made, it is only natural to wish that something about them was different, perhaps a facial characteristic, an item of clothing, or simply that they would look better in an alternative colour or material. Maybe the hair should be dark instead of fair. These are all matters of personal taste and preference. With your own doll-making, you can use whatever materials you want, and indulge a whim or a fancy.

The world of today is greatly changed from that of our Victorian ancestors: it provides plenty of inspiration for dolls of all varieties, suitable for boys as well as girls, and most people nowadays are aware of the costumes and customs of other nations all around the globe. A strong traditional theme runs throughout this book, with most of the dolls shown in these pages having their origins in folklore and fairy tales, for these are always the most popular of children's stories.

Of the dolls themselves, there are five different sizes, including the rather intriguing topsy-turvy doll, which can be turned inside-out to reveal two different expressions or personalities. You will find that safety is an important consideration in all aspects of the work, from the embroidering of the dolls' features to the avoidance of hazardous small trimmings whenever the finished rag doll is intended for a small child.

Within the instructions, repetition is present throughout, so that each doll can be made as an individual item without constantly having to refer to other sections elsewhere in the book. Material dimensions are given in metric and imperial, and you are recommended to work in either one or the other, for if you try to convert back and forth, small discrepancies will occur. Measurements are usually quoted on the generous side, so you will probably accumulate lots of trimmings and scraps, but these always have a use eventually!

Nothing now remains but to start your doll-making. I hope you will derive as much pleasure from making them as I have, and that the resulting rag dolls provide hours of fun and enjoyment for the children who receive them. You could even invent some characters of your own, and start a collection.

1 Materials and Techniques

MATERIALS YOU WILL NEED

Fabrics

The most wonderful thing about rag dolls is that you can make them out of literally any fabric. The body of the doll is usually made from cotton, linen, calico or felt, although you could even use curtain lining fabric. When dressing the doll, you can use any suitable fabrics you find around the home. It is certainly not necessary to buy expensive fabrics for your rag doll; should you wish, for instance, to make clothes using velvet, it will work out much cheaper to buy a velvet skirt from a charity shop or a second-hand sale.

FELT

A variety of coloured felts has been used in the making of the dolls' shoes. It is an ideal material as it leaves a nice neat

edge and stretches slightly to allow each shoe to be placed on the doll's foot. Because of the felt's ability to stretch, usually from selvedge to selvedge, always ensure that the shoe pieces are cut out facing the same direction.

FUR

When using fur fabric, you must remember that it has a pile that lies smoothly if it is stroked in one direction. Always place pattern onto fur in the direction indicated in the text.

NETTING

Netting can be purchased by the metre in most material shops, or it can be obtained in small circles, either way in an assortment of colours. Netting may be used as an alternative to lace when making the wings of the flower fairy, or it could be used as a stiff petticoat to support heavy skirt fabrics, such as the curtain velvet used for the snow child's coat.

SATIN

Satin tends to fray very easily, so when cutting out small pieces, such as the princess's waistcoat, it is advisable to add a backing using a lightweight interfacing which stops the fraying without making the material stiffer.

Hair

Double knitting yarn has been used for the hair of all the dolls in the book. Knitting yarns may vary in their thickness, depending on different makes. The colours of the yarns can, of course, be changed to any colour you choose.

Sewing Threads

The sewing threads are ordinary dressmaking polyester cotton threads in a variety of colours to suit the fabric which is being sewn.

Embroidery Silks

When buying embroidery threads, unless you do a lot of embroidery anyway, you do not need to buy the more well-known makes; quite often a small craft shop will stock a range of cheaper threads that children use when they first learn the techniques of embroidery, and you will often find suitable shades amongst those cheaper silks. Always use two strands of thread for the features unless otherwise stated.

Elastic

The elastic used in the book is of the round cord variety, as most of the hems for the costumes are just 6mm (¼in) wide. If round cord elastic cannot be found, you will need to use an elastic which is narrower than the 6mm (¼in) hem. When threading the elastic through the hems you will require two very small safety pins: place these one at each end of the elastic, then use the one safety pin to thread the elastic through the hem whilst the other acts as a stopper to prevent the elastic from disappearing inside the hem.

Lace

Lace is a very important ingredient in rag-doll making, as it has the ability to change the whole appearance of the doll. For example, in the case of the Cinderella topsy-turvy doll, when making the Cinders half of the doll, she is meant to be dirty and grubby from working hard in the kitchen, so a bright white lace trimming would look out of place. Make sure you think about how you want your doll to appear. The right choice of lace can make a considerable difference to the result: it can dress up a plain, drab gar-

ment so that it becomes a beautifully elaborate gown in which your doll can attend a ball. The types of lace in the book are of varying widths and these are listed for each particular doll.

Ribbons

Most of the ribbons used for the dolls are different widths of satin ribbon, and each of the dolls lists the colour and width applicable. To create a neat edge to satin ribbon, and to stop it from fraying, you will need to spread a little all-purpose adhesive onto the wrong side of the ribbon at the point where you will be cutting and leave the glue to dry before making the cut.

Braiding

Elaborate gold braiding adds a vital richness to the costumes of characters such as sultans, princes and princesses. Gold and silver lurex thread also makes an ideal trimming for dolls of this size.

Broderie Anglaise

Broderie anglaise can be bought as a piece of fabric, or as a narrow width of material which is used for edging or to make frills. Both varieties are sold by the metre, and are usually seen in white, although other colours are available. Broderie anglaise is used in the book for the traditional doll's mob cap and pinafore.

Stuffing

There are many different types of stuffing available for doll-making. Most of them are so good that it makes little difference to the end result which type you choose. The stuffing used for all the dolls shown in the book is a polyester type; most craft shops will help you to make the best choice.

Trimmings

When decorating your doll with beads and buttons, you must take into account the safety aspect of choosing the most appropriate trimmings. The age of the child for whom you are making the doll should play a large part in your selection. Beads and buttons can easily be

pulled off by young children, and may need to be left off altogether. On some of the smaller dolls, beads have been used to represent buttons, as you will not be able to obtain buttons small enough. Many of the dolls' hairstyles have been decorated with satin ribbon bows and roses, which are about the right size to be in proportion. The Sleeping Beauty crown and the medieval lady's hat have been made from gold and coloured pipe-cleaners, which can be obtained from craft shops. They are ideal because they can be bent into many different shapes very easily.

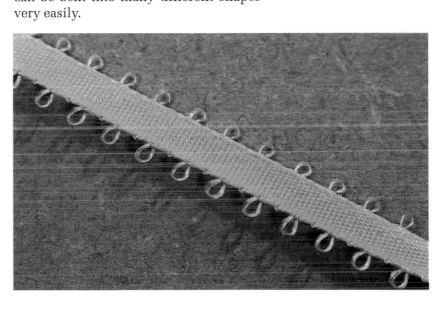

Velcro and Pop Fasteners

Velcro has become very popular for the making of dolls' clothes, since it enables children to open and close the garments themselves with much greater ease. It can be bought by the centimetre or inch and is made up of two pieces, one piece containing a surface of hooks and the other piece a surface of loops. Once pressed together, they cannot be pulled apart sideways, but are separated from one another by peeling the top away from the bottom. Pop fasteners are an alternative method, and are sewn to the garment pieces that you wish to join. One part of the fastener is sewn to one half of the garment, and the other part of the fastener is sewn to the other half. The fasteners are simply popped together to keep the garment closed.

Card

A small amount of heavy-duty card is used for the base of each foot for the larger dolls to enable them to have a solid base; it also means that the doll's shoes will fit better on each foot. Card has also been used as a template for the hair.

Fuse Wire

A length of 15-amp fuse wire is used to make the fairy doll's wings. Alternatively, you can use silver-coloured pipe-cleaners moulded to the correct shape, with a small amount of adhesive applied in order to attach the net or lace covering.

DOLL-MAKING EQUIPMENT

When making your dolls you will need some basic equipment which will help to make the sewing easier.

Sewing Machine

A sewing machine would prove very useful, especially for the larger dolls, but everything in the book can be made by hand-sewing. Indeed, all of the small dolls were sewn by hand as they are too small to go under the machine.

Needles and Pins

Make sure that all of your needles and pins have very sharp points, so that they do not damage and spoil the fabric. You will require ordinary sewing needles, embroidery needles and a darning needle, and you may also find a knitting needle very handy when stuffing your doll, as it will enable you to push the stuffing into awkward areas.

Tape Measure or Ruler

The measuring tape or ruler should have both imperial and metric measurements.

Tracing Paper

When tracing the pattern pieces, you will find that household greaseproof paper is ideal and works out a lot cheaper than buying tracing paper. To copy the patterns accurately, it is essential to use a well-sharpened pencil.

Compasses

A pair of inexpensive compasses of the type used in schools will prove very useful, but if the size of the circle that you need is identical to the diameter of a round plate or dish in the house, you may find it easier to draw a circle from around the plate than make your own pattern.

Craft Knife

A sharp craft knife is ideal for cutting out any card needed for the dolls.

Adhesive

Very little adhesive has been used in the book, as all the facial features and decorations have been embroidered or sewn onto the dolls; but should you wish to use an adhesive for added strength, a typical glue would be a clear, all-purpose adhesive.

SEWING TECHNIQUES

Safety

The safety consideration in doll-making is very important, although a lot of it is just common sense. The most important safety guide in the book is the fact that all of the dolls' faces are embroidered. Young children are always fascinated by eyes, and if these are made from felt and stuck on, they could easily be pulled off. Items such as buttons and beads can be very dangerous indeed to babies and small infants, for they could become detached and swallowed. Should you wish to make for a small child a doll which has been decorated with tiny parts, you should seek out an alternative decoration which would be safer.

Measurements

Use either metric or imperial, but not both within the same project, for if you attempt to mix the two you will discover that there are slight differences, leading to inevitable errors.

Tracing Patterns

When tracing pattern pieces, always read through carefully first so as to work out which pattern pieces are required. Make sure you transfer any pattern markings which are necessary.

Patterns

All of the patterns in the book are the correct size for the dolls, and therefore they will not need to be altered in any way, but copied exactly. Some of the pattern pieces have been drawn with a fold to enable large patterns to fit onto the page.

Rectangular Patterns

Rectangular patterns are used for many of the dolls' skirts, and are measured out and marked at the back of the fabric using a ruler and a well-sharpened pencil. Any markings to the skirts, such as where bows should be placed, are written into the relevant section for each particular doll.

Cutting Out Fabrics

When a pattern piece is marked 'on a fold', it means

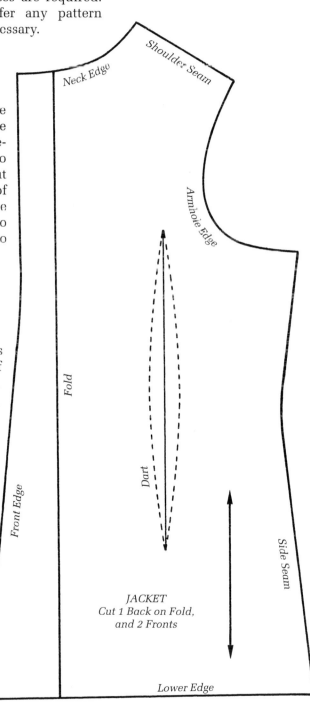

JACKET
Cut 1 Back on Fold,
and 2 Fronts

that it is to be placed on the fold of the fabric. When cutting out a pattern which states 'cut 2', always place the pattern piece onto two thicknesses of fabric, with right sides facing each other, so that you are literally reversing the pattern piece and will end up with a right and left side.

Selvedges

The selvedges are the straight of grain of the fabric. All the pattern pieces have a straight of grain arrow which indicates the correct position in which the pattern has to be placed onto the fabric; line up the arrow with the straight of grain of the fabric.

Seams

Seams are 6mm (¼in) unless otherwise stated.

Trimming or Snipping Seams

Trimming a seam means cutting away any excess fabric so as to allow the seam to sit neatly. When trimming a seam that is sewn on a curve, you will need to snip into the curved edge.

Transferring and Embroidering the Dolls' Features

Before sewing the rag doll together, you will need to transfer the features onto the front of the head using a well-sharpened pencil. When embroidering the doll's face,

fasten off the thread where it will not be noticeable, such as at the back of the head where it will eventually be covered by the doll's hair or hat. You should use a long darning needle to sew the thread through from the back of the doll's head to the front, making certain that the thread has firstly been secured at the back of the head with a knot. Change to a small embroidery needle for the features, using small back-stitches to outline the eyes, eyebrows and mouth, and satin stitch for the inner eye and nose. When you have finished with each coloured silk, take it to the back of the head, using the darning needle, and fasten it off securely.

As a final point concerning the embroidering of the eyes, note that eyelashes have been included on the features of the girl dolls but not the boy dolls, the omission being made so that the latter appear more masculine.

2 The Small Rag Doll

THE BASIC SMALL RAG DOLL

The small rag doll is an ideal doll for beginners, as it is cut out in the form of a complete body pattern, with no arm or leg joints, and therefore does not involve complicated sewing techniques. It is also the right size for children to play with. However, very young children should not be given toys which include items such as buttons or beads for decoration, since these could be pulled off or chewed and swallowed. It is therefore up to the individual to decide on the appropriateness of certain kinds of decoration, according to the child's age. All of the dolls featured in the book have embroidered faces for safety; however, this also gives them a more lifelike appearance.

MATERIALS

◆ two pieces of cream-coloured cotton fabric, each of which should measure 305 × 255mm (12 × 10in)

◆ a small quantity of stuffing

◆ an assortment of coloured silks for the doll's features.

Making the doll

Placing the right sides of the material together, cut out two body pieces from the cream-coloured cotton fabric, making sure that you transfer all markings, such as neck darts, to the wrong side of both pieces. Pencil the facial features onto the right side of one piece of fabric with a well-sharpened pencil, tracing from the relevant face pattern which matches the particular type of doll and costume that you wish to make.

Fold

SMALL DOLL
Cut 2

Dart

A   B

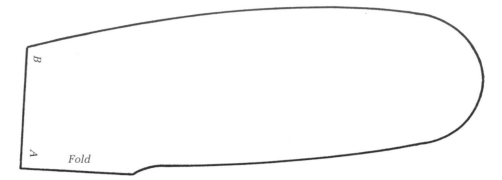

Sew the body pieces together, allowing a 6mm (¼in) seam all the way around the doll, taking care to leave a gap at the top of the doll's head between the dots so that you can turn the assembled body right side out afterwards.

Trim the seams neatly and snip away excess material from all the curved

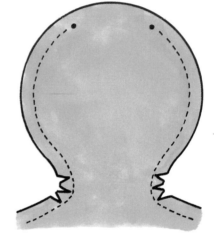

(*far right*) Snip notches around the curved edges of the neck.

(*right*) Sew along the broken line, leaving a gap between the dots.

knitting needle to push the substance fully down into the arms and legs. Fill the body and head completely until the doll is firm, and finish off by sewing up the opening at the top of the head with a neat ladder stitch.

The doll is now ready to be dressed.

edges, such as where the head meets the body at the neck. Turn the body right side out.

Stuff the body firmly with stuffing material, using the rounded end of a

(*far right*) Sew ladder stitch at the top of the head.

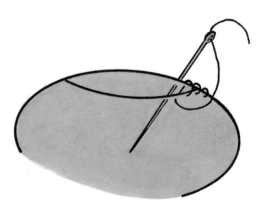

THE GYPSY RAG DOLL

The dark-haired gypsy girl in red flowing skirt is a romantic figure, a free-spirited wanderer travelling the countryside in her simple but colourful caravan.

MATERIALS

- ◆ basic small rag doll

- ◆ 255mm (10in) square of red cotton fabric

- ◆ a 255mm × 710mm (10 × 28in) piece of white cotton fabric

- ◆ a 510mm (20in) long by 38mm (1½in) wide piece of broderie anglaise lace

- ◆ 1m (39⅜in) of black narrow satin ribbon 3mm (⅛in) wide

- ◆ 1m (39⅜in) of red narrow satin ribbon 3mm (⅛in) wide

- ◆ 250mm (9⅞in) of black bias binding 25mm (1in) wide

- ◆ 500mm (19¾in) of black bias binding 13mm (½in) wide

Starting at the top of the head, sew yarn to form a spiral pattern.

The gypsy's features.

- a small amount of black double knitting yarn

- an assortment of embroidery silks

- a small amount of white narrow lace

- a 150mm (6in) square of black felt

- a short length of thin elastic

- velcro or pop fasteners

Features

Before sewing the rag doll together, transfer the standard small girl's features onto the front of the head. When deciding which coloured silks to use you will need to picture a typical gypsy. The doll featured in the book has black hair, and she has been given black eyebrows and a black outline around her eyes. She also has red lips, green eyes and a brown nose.

Hair

Using black double knitting yarn, back-stitch one end to the dot at the top of the doll's head, sew the yarn to the back of the head forming a spiral pattern, and continue sewing the yarn into place until all of the back of the head has been covered.

The remainder of the hair is made by using templates cut from card.

The fringe is made by cutting a tem-

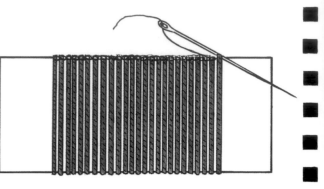

Sew yarn together securely, along one edge of the template.

plate 90mm (3½in) wide by 38mm (1½in) long. Wind the yarn around the template twenty-five times, then sew it securely together along one edge of the card

Snip yarn at the other end of the template.

before slipping the yarn off the template. This now forms the looped fringe. Fasten the sewn edge of the hair to the join along the top of the head, matching centre of fringe to centre of head, then sew in position.

Now cut out a second card template, this time measuring 125mm (5in) wide by 150mm (6in) long, and wind the yarn around this at least fifty times. Once again, sew the yarn together securely along the edge of the card and snip the yarn at the other end. Find the centre of the sewn edge of yarn and sew it to the centre of the head behind the fringe, and down the sides of the face, following the side seams.

Note that the length of each card template determines how long you want the hair to be.

Pants

Cut out two pants pieces from white cotton fabric, or a fabric of your own choice. With right sides of the fabric together, sew a 6mm (¼in) seam joining the inside leg edges. Do the same for the other leg piece. Join the pants together along the centre seams, trimming the seams neatly and snipping into the curves. Hem by hand along the lower edge of the pants pieces, taking a double 6mm (¼in) hem to form a casing for the elastic. Sew a narrow lace trimming to the lower edge of the casing and thread elastic through it, securing to the required length. Sew a double 6mm (¼in) hem along the waist edge to form a casing for the elastic, then thread the elastic through the casing and tie it to the required length. As a finishing touch, make two small red satin bows and sew these onto the centre front of each pants leg.

Blouse

From the white cotton material, or a different fabric of your choice, cut out one bodice front onto the fold in the fabric, plus two bodice backs. With right sides facing, take a 6mm (¼in) seam and sew the front and back bodice pieces together along the shoulder and side seams, trimming the seams neatly. Finish off armhole edges with a white narrow lace folded in half to form a casing, or alternatively use a bias binding. Turn a small hem along the back bodice edges to neaten. Make a frill from a strip

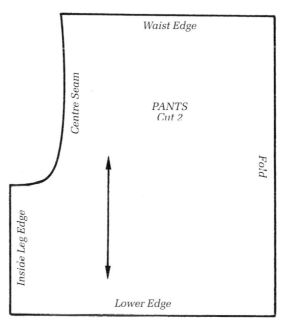

of broderie anglaise 510mm (20in) long by 38mm (1½in) wide, and sew a small hem to neaten both side edges of the frill. Sew a running stitch along the long unfinished edge of the frill and gather.

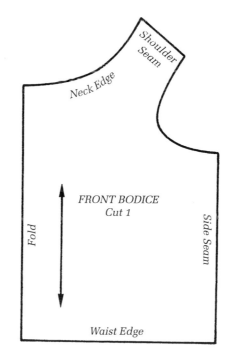

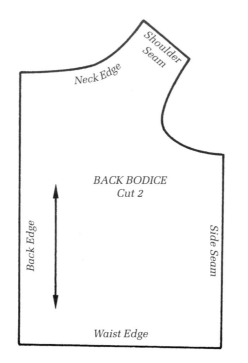

Neck Edge

Shoulder Seam

BACK BODICE
Cut 2

Back Edge

Side Seam

Waist Edge

(*right*) Cut fabric to form the back opening of the skirt between the two lines of sewing.

upper dot on the left-hand side down to the lower dot, then turn and sew up to the dot on the right-hand side. Cut between the sewing, making sure not to cut through any of the stitches. Turn the skirt to the right side and iron the back opening flat. With wrong sides together, tack the red skirt piece to the white skirt lining along the hemline and the waist edge, 3mm (⅛in) from the edge. This will hold the skirt and lining in place. To neaten the hem edge, sew a 13mm (½in) black bias binding all the way around to encase the raw edges. Using the same technique, but with a 25mm (1in) black bias binding, finish off the waist edge, overlapping one edge by 13mm (½in) for fastening. Finally, sew a pop fastener or velcro to the waistband. As a finishing touch, make and sew a small black satin bow with long ties to the centre front of the waistband.

Distribute the gathers evenly and join the frill to the neckline of the bodice, placing the wrong side of the broderie anglaise frill to the right side of the bodice neckline. Finish off the neckline with a white narrow lace folded in half to form a casing for the unfinished neck edge. Make a little red bow from narrow satin ribbon and sew it to the centre of the bodice as a finishing touch. Sew velcro or pop fasteners to the centre back pieces of the bodice.

Skirt

Cut one skirt pattern piece out of the red cotton fabric and another out of the white cotton fabric, the latter being used as a lining. Sew 3mm (⅛in) wide black satin ribbon all the way around the outer edge of the red skirt 13mm (½in) from the edge. Next, you need to make a neat opening at the waist edge. Place the right sides of the skirt pieces together and, using small stitches, sew from the

Shoes

Cut out four pieces of shoe pattern from black felt, oversew two pieces together along the curved edge, then turn the shoe pieces to the right side and place

SHOE
Cut 4

onto the doll's foot. Sew the upper edge of the shoe to the doll's foot. Finish each shoe with buckles or bows, if required.

The following items are optional and may depend on the age of the child:

Choker

Use a 3mm (⅛in) wide piece of black satin ribbon approximately 230mm (9in) long as the choker. Sew a red rose onto it as decoration, and tie or secure it at the back of the neck.

Hair Accessories

Cut two pieces of 3mm (⅛in) wide red satin ribbon, each measuring 280mm (11in) long. Make two little loops at the centre of each one, leaving the remainder to hang down at the side of the head. Secure the ribbon at the top of the head 13mm (½in) from the centre of each side. Thread beads onto a piece of black thread to match the hair, and attach them to the head in the same place as the ribbons. If your child is too young for the beaded accessories, you could always decorate the hair with red satin roses.

Bracelet

Using strong thread, place enough different coloured beads onto it to fit around the doll's arm. This could be sewn into place to prevent the bracelet from falling off. If you have a young child, you could use a very fine braiding instead (as used on the Arabian princess), which may be obtained from sewing and craft shops.

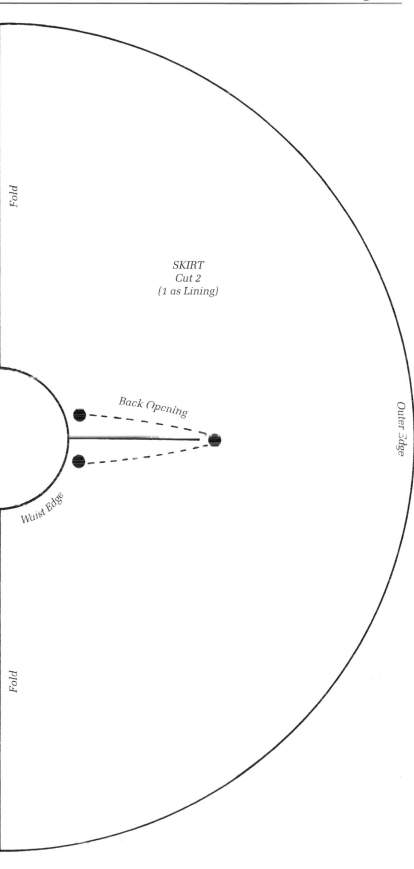

Fold

SKIRT
Cut 2
(1 as Lining)

Back Opening

Waist Edge

Outer Edge

Fold

THE CLOWN RAG DOLL

The circus clown has entertained audiences over many years by playing the fool, and his costume is usually extravagant and the face made up in bizarre patterns. Our clown has a baggy, brightly-coloured outfit, and a comical expression on his face.

MATERIALS

- basic small rag doll

- a 255 × 915mm (10 × 36in) piece of colourful cotton fabric

- 2m (78¾in) of brightly coloured satin ribbon 25mm (1in) wide

- a small amount of brightly coloured double knitting yarn

- an assortment of embroidery silks

- a 150mm (6in) square of black felt

- a short length of thin elastic

- five gold-coloured buttons

- velcro or pop fasteners

Features

Before sewing the rag doll together, transfer the clown's features onto the front of the head with a well-sharpened pencil. When studying a clown's make-up, you will see that it tends to be bold colours.

Hair

Select a colour of yarn that will complement your chosen fabric, cut approximately eighty strands measuring 50mm (2in) in length, fold each strand in half and sew it to the doll's head, following the seamline around the front of the head and down the sides of the face. Continue sewing to form a circle at the back of the head along the neckline. For the clown in the book, two rows of hair have been sewn one behind the other. There is no need to cover the back of the head, as this will be concealed by the clown's hat.

Costume

From your chosen fabric, cut out one costume front piece, placing the pattern to the fold in the fabric. Also cut out two costume back pieces, as shown on the pattern. With right sides facing, sew centre back costume pieces together between the upper and lower dots. The remaining centre back seam should be turned and sewn into a neat hem, as it will be used as the opening. Placing front and back

The clown's features.

(*left*) Sew hair to form a complete circle around the back of the head.

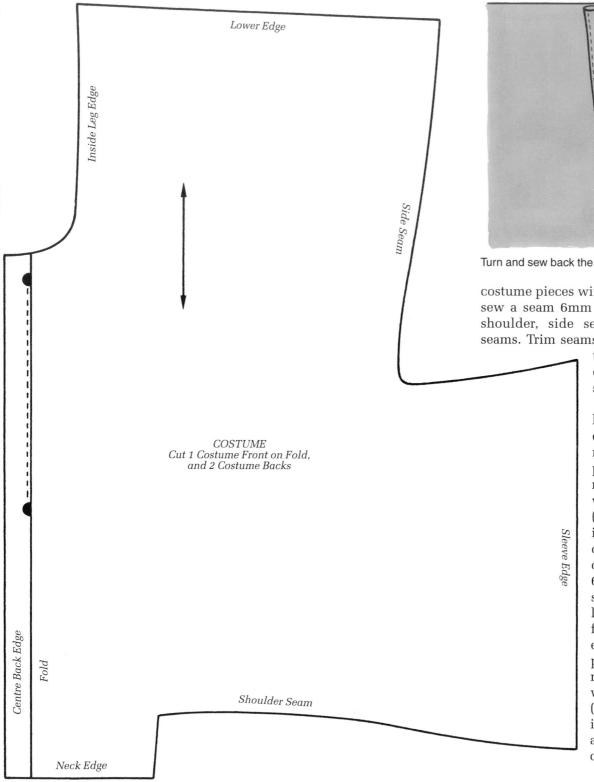

COSTUME
*Cut 1 Costume Front on Fold,
and 2 Costume Backs*

Lower Edge

Inside Leg Edge

Side Seam

Sleeve Edge

Shoulder Seam

Centre Back Edge

Fold

Neck Edge

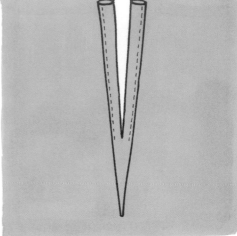

Turn and sew back the opening to neaten.

costume pieces with right sides together, sew a seam 6mm (¼in) wide along the shoulder, side seams and inside leg seams. Trim seams neatly and snip into the curves in order to enable the material to sit better.

Turn a 6mm (¼in) hem twice at the neck edge. To make the neck frill, gather a piece of yellow satin ribbon 25mm (1in) wide by 458mm (18in) long and stitch it along the neck edge of the costume. Turn over a double hem of 6mm (¼in) at the sleeve edges and lower leg edges to form a casing for the elastic. Gather up four pieces of yellow satin ribbon 25mm (1in) wide and 330mm (13in) long, attaching it to the sleeve edges and lower leg edges close to the casing. Do

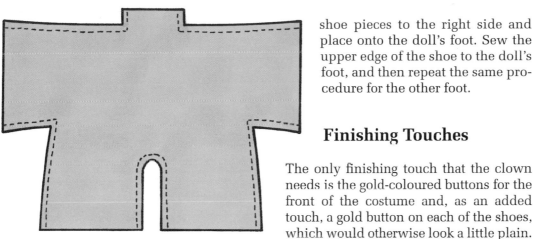

shoe pieces to the right side and place onto the doll's foot. Sew the upper edge of the shoe to the doll's foot, and then repeat the same procedure for the other foot.

(*left*) Sew the front and back pieces of the costume together along the dotted lines.

Finishing Touches

The only finishing touch that the clown needs is the gold-coloured buttons for the front of the costume and, as an added touch, a gold button on each of the shoes, which would otherwise look a little plain.

not sew the ribbon on top of the casing, as you would then be unable to thread the elastic through. Carefully thread the elastic through the casing and secure it to the required size. Sew velcro or pop fasteners along back opening to secure.

Hat

Cut the pattern piece out of your chosen fabric, ensuring that you place the centre fold of the pattern to the fold in the fabric. Sew a 6mm (¼in) seam along the back edge of the hat with right sides of the fabric together. Make a little pom-pom by folding in half and sewing ten 25mm (1in) lengths of yarn, attaching it to the hat by sewing through to the wrong side. Turn a single hem of 6mm (¼in) along the lower edge of the hat to neaten it. Place a small amount of stuffing inside the hat to allow it to stand up off the head, then sew it into place, using the hairline as a guide.

Shoes

Cut out four pieces of shoe pattern from black felt, oversew two pieces together along the curved edge, then turn the

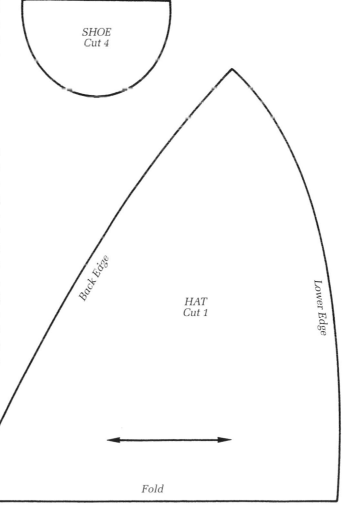

THE BRIDESMAID
RAG DOLL

Every little girl would love to be a bridesmaid, in attendance to the bride on her special day. Perhaps this doll will make a dream come true.

MATERIALS

◆ basic small rag doll

◆ a 250 × 915mm (9¾ × 36in) piece of pink satin fabric

◆ a 250 × 915mm (9¾ × 36in) piece of pink flower fabric

◆ a 100 × 305mm (4 × 12in) piece of pink cotton fabric

◆ 2.5m (98½in) of white lace 13mm (½in) wide

◆ 500mm (19¾in) of white satin ribbon 6mm (¼in) wide

◆ 500mm (19¾in) of pink narrow satin ribbon 3mm (⅛in) wide

◆ a small amount of brown double knitting yarn

◆ an assortment of coloured silks

◆ a 150mm (6in) square of pink felt

◆ a short length of thin elastic

◆ 203mm (8in) of white lace 25mm (1in) wide for bouquet

◆ silver lurex thread

◆ six white roses

◆ four pink roses

◆ velcro or pop fasteners

Features

Before sewing the rag doll together, you must transfer the bridesmaid's features onto the front of the doll's head with a pencil (as on page 14). When choosing the colours of the embroidery silks, try not to use very bright colours. The illustrated doll has been given dark brown hair, and therefore the eyebrows and the outline of the eyes should match the hair colour; the eyes are dark brown and the mouth a natural pink.

Hair

Using dark brown double knitting yarn, backstitch one end securely to the dot at the top of the doll's head, sew the yarn to the back of the head forming a spiral pattern, and continue sewing the yarn into place until all of the back of the head has been covered. For the fringe, cut a piece of card 90mm (3½in) wide by 38mm (1½in) long, take the yarn and wind it twenty-five times around the template, sew the yarn securely along one edge of the template and then snip the opposite side. Fasten the sewn edge of the hair to the central join at the top of the doll's head, matching centre of fringe to centre of head, and sew in position. For the ponytail, cut a second template measuring 63mm (2½in) wide by 90mm (3½in) long, and following the same procedure as for the fringe, wind yarn around it, this time making thirty windings, then sew along one edge, cut along the other edge, and attach the sewn edge to the head from centre top down the back.

The length of each card template determines how long you want the hair to be.

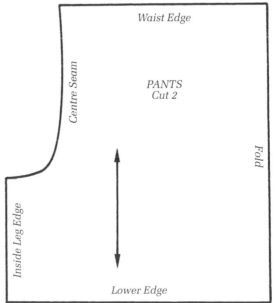

Pants

Cut out two pants pieces from white cotton fabric, or a fabric of your own choice. With right sides of the fabric together, sew a 6mm (¼in) seam joining the inside leg edges. Do the same for the other leg piece. Join the pants together along the centre seams, trimming the seams neatly and snipping into the curves. Hem by hand along the lower edge of the pants pieces, taking a double 6mm (¼in) hem to form a casing for the elastic. Sew a lace trimming to the lower edge of the casing and thread elastic through it, securing it to the required length. Sew a double 6mm (¼in) hem along the waist edge to form a casing for the elastic, then thread the elastic through the casing and fasten it to the required length.

(*left*) Starting at the top of the head, sew yarn to form a spiral pattern.

Waist Edge

Centre Seam

PANTS
Cut 2

Fold

Inside Leg Edge

Lower Edge

(*right*) Gather up thread to form a ruche and attach bows.

Dress

Cut out two skirt pieces, one from the pink satin fabric, the other from the flowered fabric, each measuring 510mm (20in) wide by 134mm (5¼in) long, and then proceed to make each skirt separately.

Starting with the underskirt, take a piece of flowered fabric and turn a double 6mm (¼in) hem along the lower edge. Sew a length of 6mm (¼in) wide white lace along the hemmed edge, allowing the scalloped edge of the lace to hang just below the hemline. Sew a silver lurex thread along the top edge of the lace for decoration. With right sides of the fabric together, sew a 6mm (¼in) seam at the centre back edges, leaving 50mm (2in) unsewn at the waist edge for the back opening, and turn a small hem to neaten the raw edges of the opening.

When making the overskirt, divide the material into eight equal segments and mark in the gathering lines with a dot, one to be placed on the hemline and the other approximately 50mm (2in)

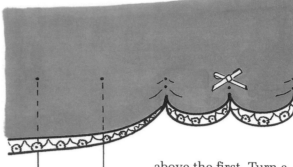

above the first. Turn a double 6mm (¼in) hem along the lower edge of the skirt, sewing a length of 6mm (¼in) wide white lace along the hem with the top of the lace to the hemline. Sew a gathering stitch from each dot to the corresponding dot at the hemline, gather up each thread to form a ruched effect, then make and sew a white satin bow to each ruche as decoration. With the right sides of the fabric together, sew a 6mm (¼in) seam at the centre back edges, leaving 50mm (2in) unsewn at the waist edge for the back opening, then turn a small hem to neaten the raw edges of the opening. Finally, place the underskirt inside the overskirt and sew a gathering stitch 6mm (¼in) from the waist edge, joining the underskirt and overskirt at the waist

Bodice

Cut out one bodice front and two bodice backs as shown in the pattern. With right sides together, take a 6mm (¼in) seam and sew the front and back bodice pieces together along the shoulder and side seams, trimming the seams neatly. Cut out and sew another bodice in the same way, to be used as a lining. Sew the bodice to the lining at centre back and neck edges. Trim the seams and clip into the corners and curves. Turn the bodice to the right side and press. Using a tacking

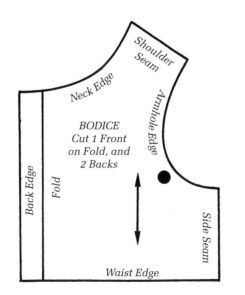

BODICE
Cut 1 Front on Fold, and 2 Backs

Shoulder Seam

Neck Edge

Armhole Edge

Back Edge

Fold

Side Seam

Waist Edge

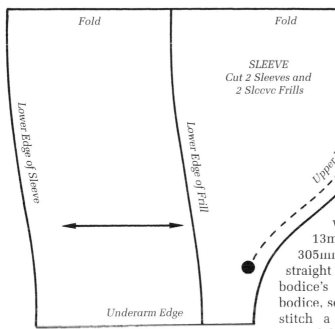

Fold

Fold

SLEEVE
Cut 2 Sleeves and
2 Sleeve Frills

Lower Edge of Sleeve

Lower Edge of Frill

Upper Edge

Underarm Edge

bodice, taking a 6mm (¼in) seam. Making sure to leave the bodice lining free, trim the waist seam neatly. Turn a 6mm (¼in) hem at the lower edge of the bodice lining and slipstitch to the waist seam of the bodice and skirt in order to encase the waist seam. Cut a piece of 13mm (½in) wide white lace 305mm (12in) long, and gather up the straight edge of the lace to fit the bodice's neckline. To decorate the bodice, sew lace along the neckline and stitch a row of silver lurex thread around the neckline as a trimming. Cut a piece of white satin ribbon 6mm (¼in) wide by 150mm (6in) long, fold the ribbon in half to find the centre, and gather with a few small stitches.

stitch, sew the bodice and the lining together at the armhole edges.

Cut out two sleeve pieces from the flowered fabric and two sleeve frills from the pink satin fabric.

To make each sleeve, place the right sides of the fabric together, sew a 6mm (¼in) seam joining the underarm edges of the sleeve, and turn a double 6mm (¼in) hem to form a casing for the elastic. Sew a piece of 13mm (½in) wide white lace to the lower edge of the sleeve. To make the frill, turn a 6mm (¼in) hem along the frill's lower edge, then sew a silver lurex thread along the frill edge to cover the sewing at the hemline. Next, place the upper edge of the sleeve and the frill together and sew a gathering stitch along the upper edge. Gather the top edges together and ease into the bodice armhole, matching up the dots. Sew the sleeve and frill into place. Thread the elastic through the sleeve casing and secure to the required length.

Gather the waist edges of the skirts, sew these to the lower edge of the

This is then sewn to the centre front of the bodice. Sew the ends of the ribbon into place at the back of the bodice, turning a small hem and slip stitching the ribbon into place at the back edges. Cut out a flower from a piece of scrap lace, or make a lace rosette to decorate the centre front of the doll's bodice. For the back bodice fastening, sew velcro or pop fasteners along the back bodice pieces.

Gather ribbon at centre front.

Shoes

Cut out four pieces of shoe pattern from the required colour of felt, oversew two pieces together along the curved edge,

SHOE
Cut 4

turn them right side out and place them onto the doll's foot. Sew the upper edge of the shoe to the foot. Finish the shoe by sewing a small bow or maybe a rose as a decoration for the centre of the shoe.

Bouquet

Cut a piece of white lace 25mm (1in) wide by 203mm (8in) long. Sew a gather stitch along the straight edge of the lace, pulling the gather stitch together to form a lace rosette. Secure tightly with a few stitches, sewing the raw edges of the lace together. This is now the base for sewing on satin ribbon and flowers of your choice.

(*right*) Satin roses and ribbon make up the bridesmaid's head-dress.

Accessories

NECKLACE

Sew and gather long edges of lace to form a rosette.

The choker necklace is a piece of 6mm (¼in) wide satin ribbon measuring

approximately 203mm (8in) long. It is gathered at the centre front and decorated with a small pearl. The ribbon is then tied at the back of the neck. You may wish to sew it into place with a few small stitches.

EARRINGS

The earrings are just pearls sewn to the side of the head with a few small secure stitches. You may need to decide whether your child is old enough for these trimmings.

HEADDRESS

The headdress for the bridesmaid is made up from small amounts of narrow ribbon and flowers sewn together and then stitched to the side of the hair.

THE FOOTBALLER RAG DOLL

Football is an obsession with many young children, and this little doll is a perfect mascot, particularly if he is dressed in their favourite team's colours.

MATERIALS

- ◆ basic small rag doll

- ◆ the footballer costume is made from a child's white polo shirt and a pair of children's red socks

- ◆ a small amount of dark brown double knitting yarn

- ◆ an assortment of coloured embroidery silks

- ◆ a 150mm (6in) square of black felt

- ◆ a short length of thin elastic

Features

Before sewing the rag doll together, you will need to transfer the footballer's features onto the front of the doll's head in pencil (as shown for Gypsy Doll on page 14). The colour of the embroidery silks that you use for his face will be dictated by the hair colour that you decide to give him. The illustrated doll has dark brown hair, so his eyebrows and eye outline are also dark brown. To brighten the features, he has green eyes, while the mouth and nose are embroidered in a biscuit brown.

Hair

Cut a card template 150mm (6in) wide by 25mm (1in) long and, using the dark brown double knitting yarn, wind it around the template until it is completely covered. Sew the yarn together securely along one edge of the template and snip the yarn at the other end. Sew the stitched edge of the yarn to the doll's head, starting at the top centre of the head and working in a spiral pattern around the back of the head. It will be necessary to make several lots of hair off the same template, sewing each successive length to the back of the head until it is completely covered.

Note that the length of the template denotes how long you wish the hair to be.

Shirt

From the red sock, cut out one front shirt piece and one back shirt piece. With right sides together, sew a 6mm

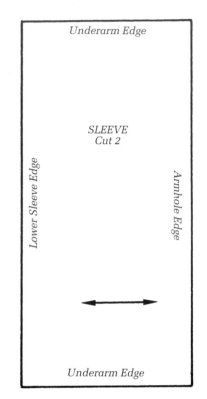

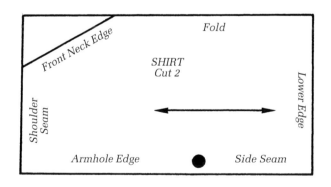

ease the sleeve into the shirt armhole and stitch, taking a 3mm (⅛in) seam around the armhole edge. Using the white ribbed collar of the polo shirt and the ribbing at the top of the red socks, cut a strip measuring 125 × 13mm (5 × ½in) from both fabrics. Sew the white fabric on top of the red, leaving an edging 3mm (⅛in) wide. Taking the double ribbed strip, sew it along the neck edge of the shirt, leaving a 3mm (⅛in) wide strip of white showing.

(¼in) seam along the shoulder and side seams. From the white polo shirt, cut out two sleeve patterns. Turn a 6mm (¼in) hem at the lower sleeve edge and, with right sides together, take a 6mm (¼in) seam along the underarm edges, then

(*right*) Sew a white strip of fabric onto the red strip, leaving a narrow edge.

3mm (⅛in)

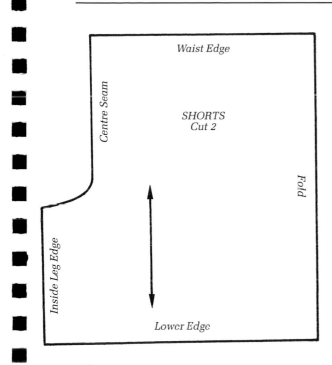

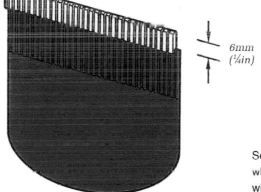

edge of the sock. Cut out a strip from the ribbed polo shirt measuring 75mm (3in) long by 13mm (½in) wide and, with right side of sock facing, place the white ribbed strip along the upper edge of the sock, overlapping the sock edge by 6mm (¼in). Sew into place with the right sides together. Now, with right sides facing, sew the inside leg edges of the sock together up as far as the beginning of the ribbing, then turn the sock to the right side, and oversew the red and white ribbing neatly together.

Shorts

The footballer's shorts are made from the white polo shirt. Cut out two shorts pieces from the fabric and, with right sides together, sew a 6mm (¼in) seam joining the inside leg edges. Repeat the same procedure for the other leg. Taking a 6mm (¼in) seam, join the shorts pieces together along the centre seam, trimming neatly and snipping into the curved edges. Cut a strip of red sock material 75mm (3in) long by 19mm (¾in) wide, sewing under 3mm (⅛in) along both long edges to avoid fraying. Sew down the side of the shorts to give a stripe; repeat on the other leg. Turn and sew a double 6mm (¼in) hem along the lower leg edge. Sew a double 6mm (¼in) hem along the waist edge to form a casing, then thread elastic through and secure it to the required length.

Socks

Cut out two sock patterns from the red sock fabric, making sure to match the upper leg edge of the pattern to the ribbed

Sew the right sides of the white and red sock together with a narrow overlap.

Football Boots

Cut out four pieces of the football boot pattern from the black felt. Oversew two pieces together along the curved edge, then turn the boot pieces to the right side and fit the boot onto the doll's foot. Sew it in place by its upper edge. Finish the football boot by using some white embroidery thread to sew a few markings along the front to represent bootlaces.

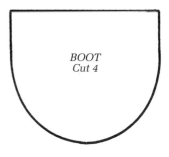

THE GUARDSMAN RAG DOLL

The guardsman, resplendent in his smart uniform, is a familiar sight in London, standing outside his sentry box or marching in the ceremonial Changing of the Guard.

MATERIALS

- ◆ basic small rag doll

- ◆ a 255mm (10in) square of black felt

- ◆ a 255mm (10in) square of red felt

- ◆ a 100 × 203mm (4 × 8in) piece of black fur fabric

- ◆ 305mm (12in) of black satin ribbon 6mm (¼in) wide

- ◆ 305mm (12in) of red narrow satin ribbon 3mm (⅛in) wide

- ◆ 250mm (9¾in) of white narrow satin ribbon 3mm (⅛in) wide

- ◆ 150mm (6in) of white satin ribbon 6mm (¼in) wide

- ◆ an assortment of coloured embroidery silks

- ◆ gold lurex thread

- ◆ thirteen small gold-coloured beads

- ◆ six small elongated gold-coloured beads

Features

Before sewing the rag doll together, transfer the guardsman's features onto the front of the head in pencil (as shown for Gypsy Doll on page 14). When choosing the coloured silks you wish to use, you will not be restricted by the need to match the colour of the hair as this will not be seen beneath the bearskin on his head. The illustrated doll has a caramel-coloured nose and mouth, the eyes and eyebrows are outlined in a darker brown and his eyes are blue.

Trousers

Cut out two trouser pieces from the black felt. Mark the centre side of the leg and sew the 3mm (⅛in) wide red satin ribbon down the side of the trousers. Turn under and sew a 6mm (¼in) hem along the lower edge and, with right sides of the fabric together, sew a 6mm (¼in) seam joining the inside leg edges. Do the same for the other leg. Join the trouser pieces together along the centre seams, taking a 6mm (¼in) allowance. Place the trousers onto the doll and make a tuck in the front along the waist edge on both sides of the centre seam.

Jacket

From the piece of red felt, cut out two jacket front pieces and one jacket back piece. With the right sides of the jacket pieces facing, allow a 6mm (¼in) seam and sew the front and back jacket pieces together along the shoulder and side seams. Sew a small strip of 3mm (⅛in) wide white satin ribbon along the shoulder seam. From the remaining red felt, cut out two sleeve pieces, decorate the lower sleeve edge with black and white ribbon, and sew the 6mm (¼in) wide black satin ribbon so that the lower edge of the ribbon lines up with the lower sleeve edge. Taking the 3mm (⅛in) wide white satin ribbon, sew it directly above the black ribbon to form a band, then, placing the right sides of the sleeve pieces together, sew a 6mm (¼in) seam joining the underarm edges of the sleeves. With the right sides of the fabric facing, ease the upper sleeve edge into the jacket armhole, then, taking a 6mm (¼in) seam, sew the sleeve and the jacket together.

Turn and sew a 6mm (¼in) hem around the jacket, which will neaten all the remaining raw edges. From a piece of 6mm (¼in) wide black satin ribbon, form a casing for the jacket neckline, by folding the ribbon in half lengthways and sewing it around the neck, thereby enclosing the raw edges. To decorate the jacket, sew nine gold-coloured beads in a row to represent buttons down the front of the left side of the jacket, then, taking two elongated gold beads, sew them to the centre front of the collar. Sew two gold beads to each sleeve above the ribbon. Place the jacket onto the doll and sew it into

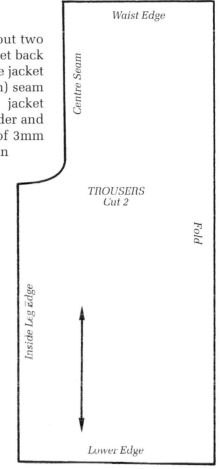

Waist Edge

Centre Seam

TROUSERS
Cut 2

Fold

Inside Leg Edge

Lower Edge

(*left*) Make a tuck on each side of the centre front seam.

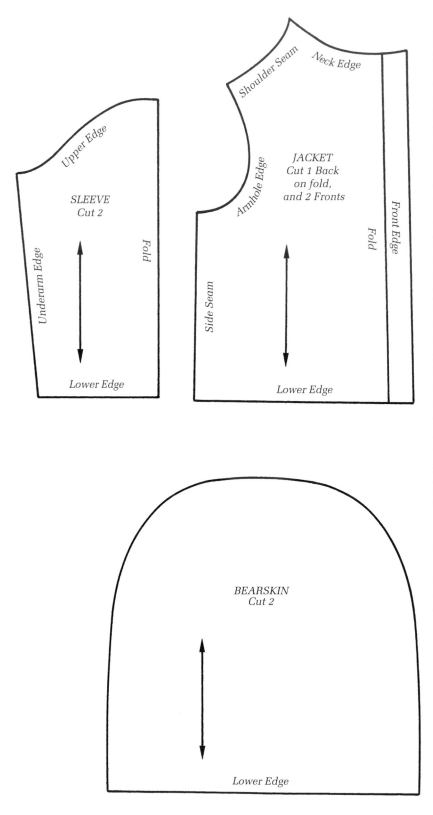

place along the front opening down as far as the waistline. Take the 150mm (6in) length of 6mm (¼in) wide white satin ribbon, and sew onto this at the centre front four gold elongated beads to form a buckle. Attach the ribbon around the waist with a few stitches at the back of the doll.

Bearskin

Taking the black fur fabric, cut out two hat pieces, making sure that the fur pile of the fabric goes from the top of the hat to the bottom. Placing the fur fabric pieces together, sew a 6mm (¼in) seam around the curved edges of the hat, tucking in any loose fur. Turn the hat to the right side; using a needle or a pin, free any fur pile that has become trapped in the seam. To make the chin strap, you will need to cut six 150mm (6in) strands of gold lurex thread. Knot the strands together at one end and then divide into three sets of two, and plait them to form the strap. When the plait is finished, knot the other end and join the plait to the inside of the hat at both side seams. Decorate with a feather.

Shoes

Cut out four pieces of shoe pattern from the black felt. Oversew two of the pieces together along the curved edge, then turn the shoe pieces to the right side and place onto the doll. Sew the upper edge of the shoe to the doll's foot.

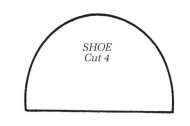

THE FLOWER FAIRY RAG DOLL

Perhaps there really are fairies at the bottom of the garden, playing hide and seek amongst the flowers when nobody is looking.

MATERIALS

- basic small rag doll

- a 255 × 203mm (10 × 8in) piece of cream-coloured cotton fabric

- 1m (39⅜in) of peach lace 100mm (4in) wide

- 500mm (19¾in) of cream lace 75mm (3in) wide

- 500mm (19¾in) of narrow cream lace 13mm (½in) wide

- 150mm (6in) of cream ribbon 13mm (½in) wide

- a small amount of dark brown double knitting yarn

- an assortment of embroidery silks

- a 150mm (6in) square of cream felt

- twelve assorted peach and cream satin roses

- silver lurex thread

- a small amount of 15-amp fuse wire or silver pipe-cleaners

- a short length of thin elastic

- velcro or pop fasteners

Features

Before sewing the rag doll together, you will need to transfer the flower fairy's features onto the front of the head in pencil (as shown for the Gypsy Doll on page 14). When deciding on the required embroidery silks for the face, you should choose those most suitable for the doll's colouring. The colour of the eyebrows and eye outline will be determined by the colour of the yarn chosen for the fairy doll's hair. The doll shown in the book has dark brown hair, which would suggest that a brighter colour is used for the eyes to add more colour to the face. Use a dusky pink thread to outline the mouth and a light brown for the nose.

Hair

Using a dark brown double knitting yarn, backstitch one end to the dot at the top of the doll's head, sew the yarn to the back of the head forming a spiral pattern, and continue sewing the yarn into place until all of the back of the head has been covered.

The remainder of the hair is made by using templates cut from card. The fringe is made by cutting a template 50mm (2in) wide by 38mm (1½in) long. Wind the yarn around the template six times, fasten together along one edge with a few stitches and slip the yarn from the template to form loops. Make another five bunches of loops in the same way and sew them to the front of the doll's head to form a fringe.

Starting at the top of the head, sew yarn to form a spiral pattern.

Now cut out a second card template, this time measuring 125mm (5in) wide by 150mm (6in) long, and wind the yarn around it at least fifty times. Once again, sew the yarn together securely along the edge of the card, and this time snip the yarn and sew it to the centre of the head behind the fringe, and down the sides of the face, following the side seams. Take three strands of yarn from the front of the head on both right and left sides and plait them, then take both plaits to the back of the head and fasten them together with a bow and rosebud. Place five satin rosebuds along the top of the head to form a headdress.

Note that the length of each card template determines how long you wish the hair to be.

Pants

Cut out two pants pieces from the cream-coloured cotton fabric, placing the fold indicated on the pattern to the fold in the fabric. Taking one leg piece, and with right sides of the fabric together, sew a

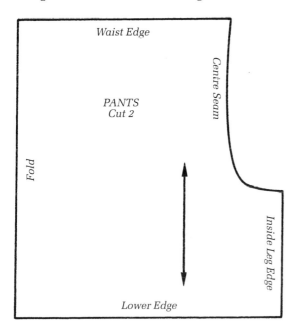

Waist Edge

Centre Seam

PANTS
Cut 2

Fold

Inside Leg Edge

Lower Edge

6mm (¼in) seam joining the inside leg edges. Do the same for the other leg piece. Join the pants pieces together along the centre seams, trim away the seams neatly and snip along the curved edge. Sew a double 6mm (¼in) hem along the lower edge of the pants pieces to form a casing for the elastic. Sew a narrow lace trimming to the lower edge of the casing and thread elastic through the casing, securing it to the required length. Sew a double 6mm (¼in) hem along the waist edge to form a casing for the elastic, then thread the elastic through the casing, once again fastening it to the required length.

Dress

From the cream-coloured fabric, cut out one bodice front onto the fold in the fabric and two bodice backs. With the right sides of the fabric facing, take a 6mm (¼in) seam and sew the front and back bodice pieces together along shoulder and side seams, trimming the seams neatly. Finish off the armhole edges with a narrow cream lace, folded in half to form a binding, or alternatively use a cream-coloured bias binding. Turn a small hem along the back bodice edges to neaten them, and sew pop fasteners or velcro to the centre back. Finish off the neckline, once again using a piece of narrow cream lace, folded in half to create a binding for the unfinished neck edge.

To make the skirt of the dress, cut a piece of cream-coloured lace 500mm (19¾in) long and a piece of peach-coloured lace of the same length, and place the cream lace on top of the peach lace with straight edges together. Sew a line of gather stitches along the top edge of the lace skirt, making sure to sew through both pieces of material. With right sides of the lace facing, sew a 6mm

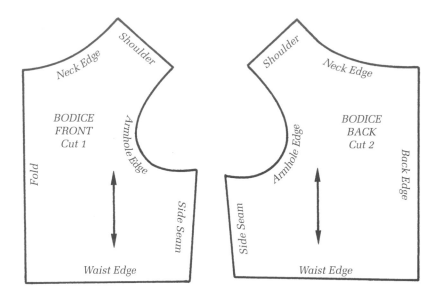

Wings

From a piece of thin fuse wire, copy the shape of the wings from the pattern, lay a piece of peach-coloured lace over the wire frame and sew it into place. Cut away any excess lace and decorate the wings with a lurex thread before sewing them firmly to the back of the doll.

Shoes

Cut out four pieces of shoe pattern from cream-coloured felt, and four pieces from peach-coloured lace. Sew the lace to the felt shoe pieces and then, with right sides together, oversew the pieces along the curved edge. Turn the shoe pieces to the right side and place them onto the doll's foot, sewing into position along the upper edge. Complete the shoe by decorating it with a thread of silver lurex sewn along the upper edge and a peach bow or rose fastened on the front, if required.

(¼in) seam joining the back skirt edges together, leaving a 38mm (1½in) opening at the waist edge. Gather up the lace and, with right sides facing, join the bodice waist edge to the skirt waist edge. For decoration, finish off the waist by sewing a 13mm (½in) wide strip of cream satin ribbon along the waist edge, and sew three assorted satin bows to one side of waist. Trim the front of the bodice with a row of pearls, and cut out some thin strips of cream and peach lace to sew along the shoulder seams; finally, sew a peach satin rose to each shoulder.

Accessories

BRACELET

A tiny scrap of silver rickrack is used to make the bracelet, with a peach thread twisted around it and sewn to the back of the arm for safety.

NECKLACE

The necklace is made from a piece of silver lurex thread and a piece of peach-coloured thread, both twisted together, and then tied at the back of the neck beneath the doll's hair.

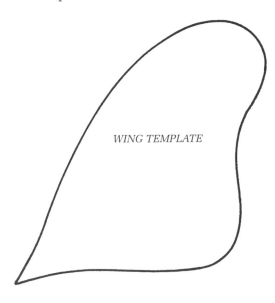

WING TEMPLATE

THE HANSEL AND GRETEL RAG DOLLS

A pair of rag dolls could be made to represent twins, a brother and sister, or simply well-known characters from children's stories. Our illustrated pair are Hansel and Gretel, but they might just as easily be Jack and Jill. With a little modification here and there, taken individually the boy doll could be Oliver Twist and the girl doll Heidi. There are all sorts of possibilities.

MATERIALS – HANSEL

- ◆ basic small rag doll

- ◆ a 254 × 458mm (10 × 18in) piece of grey corduroy fabric

- ◆ a 203 × 305mm (8 × 12in) piece of blue cotton fabric

- ◆ a 305mm (12in) square of black felt

- ◆ a small amount of light brown double knitting yarn

- ◆ an assortment of embroidery silks

Features

Before sewing the rag doll together, transfer Hansel's features onto the front of the head in pencil (as shown for the Gypsy Doll on page 14). When selecting the colours of the silks you wish to use, you will need to consider that Hansel has been given light brown hair, so the eyebrows and eye outline ought to be light brown. The nose is sewn from a caramel colour and his mouth is dusky pink.

Hair

The hair for Hansel is made by using two card templates. For the fringe cut a template measuring 50mm (2in) wide by 38mm (1½in) long, wind the yarn around the template about twenty times, sew it securely along one edge and snip the yarn at the other edge. Place the sewn edge of the hair along the centre seam of the doll's head and sew into place. For the remaining hair, cut a template 75mm (3in) wide by 90mm (3½in) long, wind the yarn around the template approximately

forty times, and once again sew the yarn firmly along one edge and snip the yarn at the other, then place the sewn edge of the hair along the centre seam and sew onto the head.

Remember that the length of each card template determines how long you want the hair to be.

Shirt

From the blue cotton fabric, cut out two shirt fronts and one shirt back placed on the fold in the fabric. With right sides facing, take a 6mm (¼in) seam and sew the front and back shirt pieces together along the shoulder and side seams, trimming the seams neatly. Cut out two sleeve pieces from the same fabric and, with the right sides facing, join the underarm seams. Turn a double 6mm (¼in) hem along the sleeve's lower edge to neaten it. Ease the sleeve into the shirt arm-

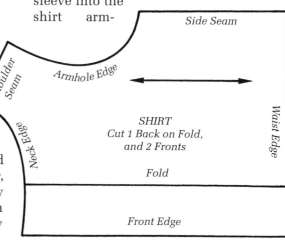

hole and sew into place taking a 6mm (¼in) seam. Take a double 6mm (¼in) hem along the front of the shirt, turning the hem towards the front of the shirt to form a decorative band at the centre front. Cut a bias strip 125mm (5in) long by 25mm (1in) wide to be used as the shirt collar. Sew the bias strip to the neckline taking a 6mm (¼in) seam, turn under the fabric along the short edge of the strip to neaten and then turn under a 6mm (¼in) hem along the strip and slip stitch the bias strip to the inside neckline to form a casing for the seam. Place the shirt onto the doll and secure the fronts into place by sewing down the centre front bands.

Trousers

Cut out two trouser pieces from the grey corduroy fabric. Turn under and sew a double 6mm (¼in) hem along the lower leg edge, then, with the right sides of the fabric together, sew a 6mm (¼in) seam joining the inside leg edges, repeating for the other leg. Join the trousers together along the centre seams, taking a 6mm (¼in) seam. Turn a 6mm hem along the waist edge. Place the trousers onto the doll and make a tuck on the waist edge on both sides of the centre seam

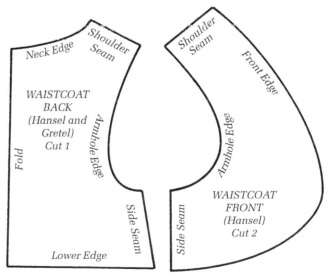

Make a tuck on each side of the centre front seam.

Waistcoat

From the black felt, cut out two waistcoat fronts and one waistcoat back. Sew a 6mm (¼in) seam joining the front and back pieces together along the shoulder and side seams, turn to the right side and place onto the doll.

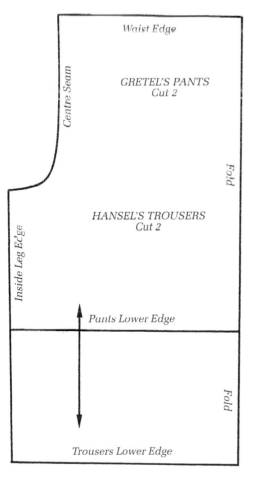

Waist Edge

Centre Seam

GRETEL'S PANTS
Cut 2

Fold

Inside Leg Edge

HANSEL'S TROUSERS
Cut 2

Pants Lower Edge

Fold

Trousers Lower Edge

Neck Edge

Shoulder Seam

Shoulder Seam

Front Edge

WAISTCOAT
BACK
(Hansel and Gretel)
Cut 1

Fold

Armhole Edge

Armhole Edge

WAISTCOAT
FRONT
(Hansel)
Cut 2

Side Seam

Side Seam

Lower Edge

Hat

From the remaining grey corduroy fabric, cut out a circle measuring 165mm (6½in) in diameter, and a strip 50mm (2in) wide by 203mm (8in) long. Sew a gathering stitch along the edge of the circle 6mm (¼in) in from the edge. Taking the corduroy strip, sew the short edges together. Gather the sewing around the circle and ease the gathers to fit into the strip. Join the strip and circle together taking a 6mm (¼in) seam, turn a 6mm (¼in) hem along the other raw edge of the strip and slip stitch into place, encasing the raw-edged seam. Turn the hat to the right side and sew into position on the doll's head.

Shoes

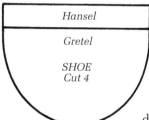

Cut out four pieces of shoe pattern from the black felt, oversew two pieces together along the curved edge, turn the shoe pieces to the right side and place the shoe onto the doll's foot. Sew the upper edge of the shoe onto the doll. Finish the shoe with a decoration of your choice.

MATERIALS – GRETEL

- basic small rag doll

- a 710 × 254mm (28 × 10in) piece of white cotton fabric

- a 458 × 100mm (18 × 4in) piece of green cotton fabric

- a 150mm (6in) square of black felt

- a 150mm (6in) square of dark green felt

- 500mm (19¾in) of cream lace 19mm (¾in) wide

- 1m (39⅜in) of white lace 13mm (½in) wide

- 500mm (19¾in) of green narrow satin ribbon 3mm (⅛in) wide

- a small amount of yellow double knitting yarn

- an assortment of embroidery silks

- a short length of thin elastic

- velcro or pop fasteners

Features

Before sewing the rag doll together, you will need to transfer Gretel's features onto the front of the head in pencil (as shown for the Gypsy doll on page 14). When deciding on the colours of embroidery thread for the face, much will depend upon the colour chosen for the hair. The illustrated doll has fair hair, and therefore the features will need to be quite pale. A light brown has been used in this instance for the eyebrows and the outlining of the eyes and also the nose; the eyes have been embroidered in an ice blue and the mouth is dusky pink.

Hair

The hair for the rag doll is made by using a card template measuring 90mm (3½in) wide and 165mm (6½in) long. Wind the yarn around the template approximately eighty times. Sew the yarn securely along one edge of the card and snip it at the other end. Open up the yarn and use the line of sewing as a parting down the centre of the back of the head and sew into place. Divide the hair on each side of the head into three equal parts and plait them together, fasten them with a small length of yarn and decorate by tying a 125mm (5in) length of green ribbon around them in a bow. The fringe is made by cutting another card template, this time measuring 90mm (3½in) wide by 25mm (1in) long. Wind the yarn around the template five times, slip it off the card and then thread another piece of yarn of the same colour through the loops and knot tightly. This now forms a bunch of

loops for the fringe. Make another identical four bunches, and then sew one set of loops to the centre of the head in front of the plaited hair, and place two more sets of loops on either side of the centre one.

Note that the length of each template denotes how long you want the hair to be.

Pants

Cut out two pants pieces from white cotton fabric. With right sides of the fabric facing, sew a 6mm (¼in) seam joining the inside leg edges. Do the same for the other leg piece. Join the pants pieces together along the centre seams, trim the seams neatly and snip into the curves. Hem by hand along the lower

edge of the pants pieces, taking a double 6mm (¼in) hem to form a casing for the elastic. Sew a narrow lace trimming to the lower edge of the casing and thread elastic through it, securing to the required length. Sew a double 6mm (¼in) hem along the waist edge to form a casing for the elastic, then thread the elastic through once again, securing it as before. A nice finishing touch is to make two small green satin bows and sew them onto the centre front of each pants leg.

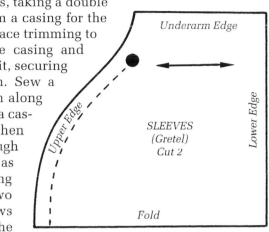

Blouse

From the white cotton fabric, cut out one bodice front onto the fold in the fabric and two bodice backs. With right sides facing, take a 6mm (¼in) seam and sew the front and back bodice pieces together along the shoulder and side

(*far left*) Snip yarn at the opposite end to the sewn edge.

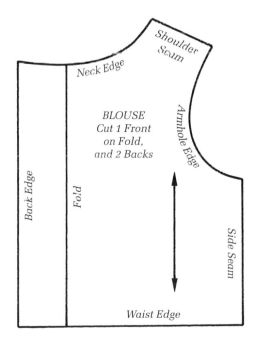

seams, trimming the seams neatly. Cut out two sleeve pieces from the white cotton fabric and, with right sides of fabric together, join the underarm seams. Turn a double 6mm (¼in) hem along the sleeve's lower edge to form a casing for the elastic, sew a 13mm (½in) wide white lace just above the casing for decoration, thread elastic through the casing and secure it to the required length.

Slip stitch bias edge to neckline.

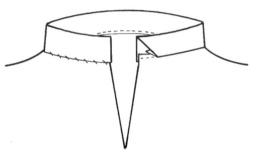

Gather along the upper edge of each sleeve between the dots as shown on the pattern, ease the sleeve into the blouse's armhole and sew into place. Trim the armhole seams neatly and oversew the raw edges. To make a stand-up collar, you will need to cut a strip of white cotton fabric on the bias, which should measure 125 × 25mm (5 × 1in). Taking a 6mm (¼in) seam, join the bias strip to the blouse neckline, making sure to turn under the raw edges of the bias strip at the back opening. Turn under a 6mm (¼in) hem along the other edge of the bias strip and slip stitch it to the inner neckline. Now, taking a piece of 13mm (½in) wide white lace, sew it to the inside of the

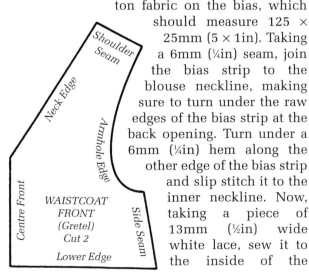

Shoulder Seam

Neck Edge

Armhole Edge

Centre Front

WAISTCOAT
FRONT
(Gretel)
Cut 2

Side Seam

Lower Edge

stand-up collar, gathering the lace as you go around and making sure to allow the lace to show over the collar. Turn a double 6mm (¼in) hem along both backs and lower edges of the blouse. Sew velcro or pop fasteners to the back opening of the blouse. Make a green satin bow to decorate the centre front of the blouse.

Skirt

Cut out a piece of green fabric measuring 458 × 100mm (18 × 4in). Turn a double 6mm (¼in) hem along the lower edge of the skirt and sew a 19mm (¾in) wide piece of cream lace 25mm (1in) above the hemline. Placing right sides of fabric together, take a 6mm (¼in) seam along the centre back seam and trim neatly. Turn a double 6mm (¼in) hem along the waist edge to form a casing for the elastic. Thread elastic through it and secure to the required length.

Waistcoat

From the dark green felt, cut out two waistcoat fronts and one waistcoat back. Sew a 6mm (¼in) seam joining the front and back pieces together along the side and shoulder seams, then turn to the right side and place onto the rag doll. Close the front opening with a few crisscross stitches.

Shoes

Cut out four pieces of shoe pattern from the black felt, oversew two pieces together along the curved edge, turn the shoe pieces to the right side and place the shoe onto the doll's foot, sewing it into place along the upper edge. Finish the shoe with a decoration of your choosing.

Fold

MEDIUM DOLL
Cut 2

Dart

A

B

3 The Medium Rag Doll

THE BASIC MEDIUM RAG DOLL

Many older children will have discovered the world of books and storytelling, and the medium rag doll should appeal to their young imaginations. The characters for this size of doll have been taken from well-known folk tales.

The medium rag doll thus being aimed at the slightly older child, it can be more elaborately dressed and given adornments such as necklaces, tiaras and swords; it should also be possible for you to sew on sequins and pearls, or any other trimmings that seem desirable.

The doll's features are again hand-embroidered to allow each to have a character of its own.

A *B*

Fold

MATERIALS

◆ two pieces of cream-coloured cotton fabric, each of which should measure 458 × 356mm (18 × 14in)

◆ a small quantity of stuffing

◆ an assortment of different coloured embroidery silks for the doll's features

Making the Doll

Placing the right sides of the material together, cut out two body pieces from the cream-coloured cotton fabric (unless the nationality of the doll makes it necessary to use a darker coloured material), making sure that you transfer all markings, such as neck darts, to the wrong side of both pieces. The procedure is identical to that of the basic small rag doll, except that the pieces are somewhat larger. Mark out the facial features onto the right side of the fabric with a well-sharpened pencil, noting that the face pattern should match the type of doll and costume that you have chosen to make.

Sew the body pieces right-sides together, leaving a gap at the top of the doll's head between the dots. Trim the seams neatly and clip the curved edges to enable the material to sit properly.

Turn the sewn body pieces the right way round and begin to stuff the doll, using small amounts of stuffing at a time so that the arms and legs can be filled more easily and thoroughly. Use the rounded end of a knitting needle for this purpose. Stuff firmly, but do not overstuff, as this will only make

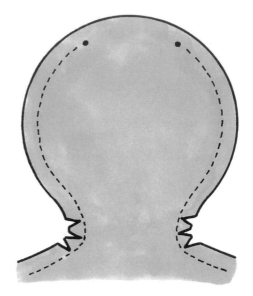

Sew along the broken line, leaving a gap between the dots. Snip notches around the curved edges of the neck.

the doll too rigid. When you are satisfied that the doll is stuffed sufficiently, sew up the opening at the top of the head with a neat ladder stitch.

The doll is now ready to be dressed.

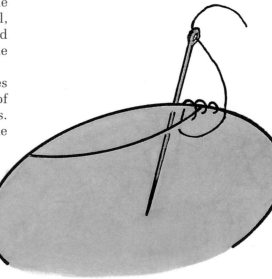

Sew ladder stitch at the top of the head.

THE BRIDE RAG DOLL

The bride doll never goes out of fashion; a wedding day is perhaps the only occasion when you can dress up in a beautiful gown. But you can really enjoy yourself elaborately dressing up the bride doll for her own special day.

MATERIALS

- ◆ basic medium rag doll

- ◆ a 500 × 915mm (19¾ × 36in) piece of white satin fabric

- ◆ 1.5m (59in) of white lace 125mm (5in) wide

- ◆ 2.5m (98½in) of white lace 90mm (3½in) wide

- ◆ 1.5m (59in) of white narrow lace 13mm (½in) wide

- ◆ 250mm (9⅞in) of white satin ribbon 16mm (⅝in) wide

- ◆ 500mm (19¾in) of white narrow satin ribbon 3mm (⅛in) wide

- ◆ 500mm (19¾in) of green narrow satin ribbon 3mm (⅛in) wide

- ◆ 1.5m (59in) of decorative ribbon (pleated ribbon was used here)

- ◆ a small amount of cream-coloured double knitting yarn

- ◆ a selection of coloured embroidery silks

- ◆ silver lurex thread

- ◆ one packet of pearls

- ◆ ten medium white roses

- ◆ eight small pink roses

- ◆ a short length of thin elastic

- ◆ velcro or pop fasteners

Features

Before sewing the rag doll together, transfer the bride's features onto the front of the head with a well-sharpened pencil. The coloured silks for your bride doll should keep to the natural tones, as any bold or bright colours will appear too harsh.

Hair

Using a cream-coloured double knitting yarn, backstitch one end securely to the dot on the top of the back of the head, sew the yarn to the back of the head forming a spiral pattern, and continue sewing the yarn into place until the back of the head is entirely covered.

To make the fringe curls, wind the yarn ten times around the top of your middle finger, thread a piece of yarn of the same colour through the loops and knot it tightly to form a bunch of curls; repeat this procedure to make four or five more curl clusters for the fringe. Sew the fringe to the top of the doll's head at the centre front.

For the remaining hair, cut a card template 75mm (3in) wide by 255mm (10in) long, marking in and cutting three 6mm (¼in) wide slits, one at the centre of the template and one at each end, set 25mm (1in) in from the edge. Wind the yarn around the template thirty times, and sew it together through the middle slit to form a centre parting. Taking pieces of matching yarn, pass through each of the outer slits and tie together to form two bunches. Cut through the card and slip the yarn from the template. Now sew the centre parting to the front of the head

The bride's features.

Starting at the top of the head, sew yarn to form a spiral pattern.

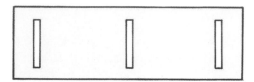

Template pattern.

and down the centre back, covering the top part of the spiral, and finally fasten the bunches to the sides of the head.

Pants

Cut out two pants pieces from white cotton fabric, or a fabric of your own choice and, with right sides together, sew a 6mm (¼in) seam joining the inside leg edges; repeat for the other leg. Join the pants together along the centre seams, trim the seams neatly and snip into the curves. Hem by hand along the lower edge of the pants pieces to form a casing for the elastic. Sew a lace trimming to the lower edge of the casing and thread a thin piece of elastic through the casing, fastening it to the required length. Hem the waist edge to form a casing for the elastic, and once again pass the elastic through and secure.

Bodice

Cut out one bodice front and two bodice backs, as shown on the pattern. With the right sides together, take a 6mm (¼in) seam and sew the front and back bodice pieces together along the shoulder and side seams, trimming the seams neatly. Cut out and sew another bodice in the same way, to be used for the lining. Sew the bodice to the lining at the centre back and neck edges. Trim the seams and clip into the corners and curves. Turn the bodice to the right side and press. Using a tacking stitch, sew the bodice and the lining together at the armhole edges.

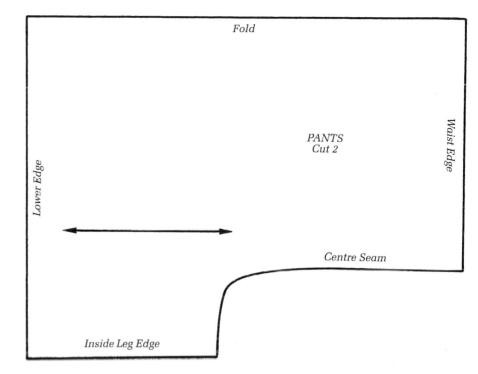

Sleeves

Cut out two sleeve pieces as shown on the pattern and, with right sides together, join the underarm seams. To form a casing for the elastic, turn a double 6mm (¼in) hem at the lower edge of the sleeve, sew lace or trimming to it and thread elastic through to fit. Gather along the armhole edge of each sleeve between the dots, as shown on the pattern, matching the sleeve seams to the side seams of the bodice, and gather the top of the sleeve to fit into the armhole. Sew the sleeve into place. Neatly trim the seams and oversew the raw edges.

Dress

Cut out a piece of satin 242 × 710mm (9½in × 28in), and sew a piece of lace measuring 710mm (28in) long by 90mm (3½in) wide along the waist edge of the skirt 25mm (1in) from the waistline. Turn a 6mm (¼in) hem at the lower edge of the skirt piece and sew a length of white narrow lace onto the right side of the skirt to cover any sewing; this will also give the skirt a nice finish. Gather a piece of lace 1,220mm (48in) long by 90mm (3½in) wide and sew into place along the skirt's hemline, leaving the shaped edge of the lace to hang just below the hem. Sew the pleated ribbon and lace, or a trimming of your own choice, over the gathered edge of the lace. The doll shown in the book has been decorated with pearls sewn on to lace. With right sides together, join the back seam, leaving an opening of 50mm (2in) at the waist edge, and turn a small hem at the opening to neaten. Gather the waist edge of the skirt and sew to the lower edge of the bodice, taking a 6mm (¼in) seam. Neatly trim the seam, making sure to leave the bodice lining free. Turn under 6mm (¼in) at the lower edge of the bodice lining and slip stitch the waist edge of the bodice lining and skirt together, encasing the waist seam.

Gather a piece of white narrow lace measuring 255mm (10in) long and sew it into place along the bodice's edge. Using a silver lurex thread, trim along the neck between the neck edge and lace. Cut one

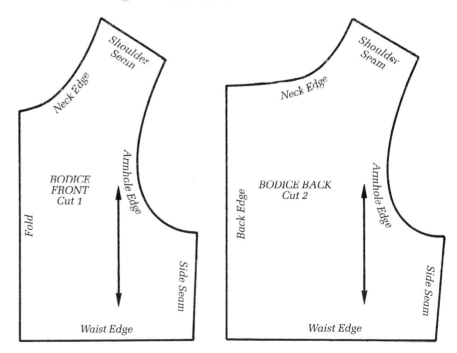

SLEEVE
Cut 2

Upper Edge

Fold

Underarm Edge

Lower Edge

piece of 13mm (½in) wide white lace 230mm (9in) long, place one end of the lace to the left side of the bodice back at the neck edge, sew into place along the bodice back over the shoulder seam and down to the centre front of the bodice. Fold the lace at the waist edge and begin to sew the lace into place up the right side of the bodice over the shoulder seam to the back right edge. Fasten off the lace neatly. Using the silver lurex thread as decoration, sew the thread along the lace as a finishing touch.

To decorate the waistline, cut a 178mm (7in) long piece of the 16mm (⅝in) wide white satin ribbon and gather the centre of the ribbon with a few small stitches. Next, make a rosette, using a piece of white lace 13mm (½in) wide by 150mm (6in) long. Gather up the straight edge of the lace, pulling it to form a circular rosette pattern, then decorate the centre of the rosette with a rose or a pearl cluster, and sew the rosette to the centre of the ribbon. Place the ribbon around the doll's waist and sew into position along the back edges of the bodice. Sew velcro or pop fasteners to the bodice back opening.

Veil

Cut two pieces of white lace measuring 394mm (15½in) long by 125mm (5in) wide which will be used as the long under veil. Join together the two pieces of lace by overlapping the

Make tucks in upper veil to allow it to fit to the under veil.

long straight edges and sewing them neatly, then turn over a 6mm (¼in) hem at the lower edge. Cut a piece of white lace 406mm (16in) long by 125mm (5in) wide which will be used as the short upper veil. Turn a 6mm (¼in) hem on both raw edges of the lace to neaten. Sew the short edges of the lace to the top side edges of the under veil. Make a few tucks in the upper veil so that it can fit onto the top edges of the under veil, and, gathering both pieces of veil together, pull tightly and sew them securely onto the top of the doll's head. Sew or glue a few roses into place at the front of the veil to form a headdress.

Shoes

Cut out four pieces of shoe pattern from the required colour felt, oversew two pieces together along the curved edge, turn the shoe pieces right side out and place onto the doll's foot, sewing into place along the upper edge. Finish the shoes with roses, bows or even a small amount of narrow lace and some silver lurex thread.

SHOE
Cut 4

Pleated ribbon sewn over gathered lace.

Accessories

NECKLACE

Make a pearl necklace by threading pearls onto a piece of cotton and fastening it at the back of the neck. Alternatively, you could make a silver choker instead of a pearl necklace.

BOUQUET

To make the bouquet, twist a number of white and pink roses together to form whatever shape you require, finishing off with white and green narrow satin ribbon made into loops and allowed to hang loose.

THE PRINCE CHARMING RAG DOLL

Every little girl must at some time dream of a prince who will carry her away to his castle where they will live happily ever after. The prince in this book is made so that he can be played with together with the Cinderella topsy-turvy doll.

MATERIALS

- ◆ basic medium rag doll

- ◆ a 228 × 255mm (9 × 10in) piece of lilac satin fabric

- ◆ 250mm (9¾in) of purple velvet, or a scrap piece measuring approximately 330 × 356mm (13 × 14in)

- ◆ 500mm (19¾in) of white lace 38mm (1½in) wide

- ◆ 750mm (29½in) of white lace 19mm (¾in) wide

(*right*) Back of hair tied with ribbon to form a ponytail.

- 500mm (19¾in) of lilac satin ribbon 6mm (¼in) wide

- 1m (39⅜in) of silver braiding

- a 150mm (6in) square of black felt

- a small amount of black double knitting yarn

- an assortment of coloured embroidery silks

- a small amount of white nylon petticoat fabric

- two satin bows with pearls

- a small piece of silver kid fabric or silver card

- a short length of thin elastic

Features

Before sewing the rag doll together, transfer Prince Charming's features onto the front of the head (as shown for Bride Doll on page 46). In choosing the embroidery silks, take into account that it is a male doll and should therefore have more subtle shades. The illustrated doll has black hair, so has been given black eyebrows and a black outline around the eyes; the choice for the eyes is blue, with the nose and mouth sewn in a warm brown silk.

Hair

Using black double knitting yarn and a card template measuring 63mm (2½in) wide by 100mm (4in) long, wind the yarn around the template forty times. Sew the yarn together along one edge, and cut it at the opposite end. Place the sewn edge of the hair to the back of the head, roughly

Template pattern.

halfway down, tie it into a pony tail with a lilac satin ribbon and sew the hair into place at the back of the neck.

Cut a second card template, this time measuring 90mm (3½in) wide by 150mm (6in) long, then mark and cut out three 6mm (¼in) wide slits, one positioned at the centre of the template, and the other two set one at either end of the template, 25mm (1in) in from the edge. Wind the yarn around the template twenty times, securing the hair by sewing the yarn together through all three slits; this will provide for a parting along the centre of the hair and the rolled hair which is sewn to the sides of the head. Cut away the card, and sew the centre parting to the centre dot at the front of the head, and along the centre back, covering the head where the top of the ponytail is already sewn.

Make another section of hair in the same way as the last one by using a third template which is 25mm (1in) shorter overall and which will enable the rolled curls on each side of the head to rest one on top of the other, in a similar fashion to the wig worn by a court judge.

The curls at the front of the head are made by winding yarn around the middle finger twenty times, securing the loops with a few firm stitches and sewing the curls to the centre front of the head at the front of the parting.

Stockings

Cut out four stocking pieces from a piece of white nylon fabric such as that used for petticoats, making certain that the fabric stretches across the width of the leg. With right sides together, sew around the stocking pieces, then turn right side out and place the stocking onto the doll's leg, sewing it into place at the upper leg.

Pants

From the lilac-coloured satin, cut out two pants pieces placed on the fold of fabric, as shown on the pattern. With right sides together, sew a 6mm (¼in) seam joining the inside leg edges, and repeat the same procedure for the other leg piece. Join the pants pieces along the centre seam, trim the seams neatly and snip into the curves. Hem by hand along the lower edge of the pants pieces to form a casing for the elastic. Sew a 13mm (½in) wide piece of white lace along the upper edge of the casing, thread a narrow piece of elastic through the casing and secure the elastic to the required length. Decorate along the lace with a satin bow and pearl. Sew a double 6mm (¼in) hem along the waist edge to form a casing for the elastic, thread the elastic through the casing and fasten it to the required length.

Jacket

From the purple-coloured velvet, cut out two jacket front pieces and one jacket back piece, making sure to transfer all relevant markings from the pattern. Sew darts in place as indicated, one down each front and two down the back of the jacket. With right sides of fabric together, allow a 6mm (¼in) seam and sew the front and back jacket pieces together along the shoulder and side seams. Trim the seams neatly. There are certain velvet fabrics that may fray, and you will therefore need to blanket stitch along the raw edges. From the remaining velvet, cut out two sleeve pieces. Turn and sew a 6mm (¼in) hem along the lower sleeve edge, gather a piece of white lace 19mm (¾in) wide by 203mm (8in) long and sew it to the inside of the lower edge of the sleeve so that it looks like a frilled lace cuff, and sew a

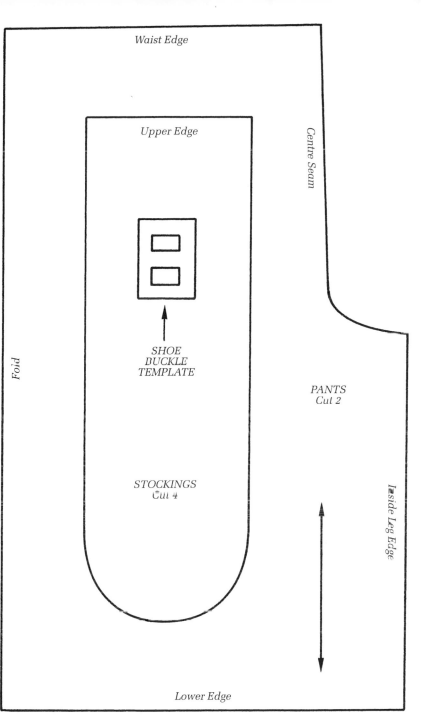

Neck Edge

Shoulder Seam

Armhole Edge

Fold

Dart

Front Edge

Side Seam

JACKET
*Cut 1 Back on Fold,
and 2 Fronts*

Lower Edge

Underarm Edge

Upper Edge

Lower Edge

SLEEVE
Cut 2

Fold

piece of silver braiding along the lower sleeve 3mm (⅛in) away from the sleeve edge.

With right sides of the fabric together, sew a 6mm (¼in) seam joining the underarm edges of the sleeve together, then ease the upper sleeve edge into the jacket armhole; sew sleeve and jacket together taking a 6mm (¼in) seam, trim the seam neatly and blanket stitch the raw edges to prevent them from fraying. Turn and sew a double 6mm (¼in) hem to neaten all remaining raw edges around the jacket.

Cut a piece of velvet on the bias, 38mm (1½in) wide by 125mm (5in) long, which will be used as a collar for the jacket. With right sides of fabric facing, sew a 6mm (¼in) seam joining the bias strip to the jacket's neck edge, turning under any excess bias fabric at the front edges, then turn a 6mm (¼in) hem along the remaining raw edge of bias strip and sew it into place along the inside of the jacket

Silver kid buckles sewn to front of shoe.

at neck edge. Sew a silver braiding 3mm (⅛in) in from the edge along the collar, jacket front edge and along the hemline. Place the jacket onto the doll and sew collar and front opening together down as far as the waistline.

To make a frill at the front of the jacket, cut two 75mm (3in) strips of 19mm (¾in) wide white lace, neaten the raw edges of the lace and gather along its straight edge, sewing to the front of the jacket.

Shoes

From the black felt, cut out two standard shoe shapes for the back of the shoe and two shoe fronts from the Prince Charming shoe pattern. Oversew front and back pieces together along the curved edge, turn the shoe pieces to the right side and place the shoe onto the doll's foot, sewing it into position along the upper edge. The buckles used in the book are made from a small scrap of silver kid material; cut out the two silver buckles as shown on the pattern and sew them onto the centre front of each shoe.

SHOE
*Cut 4
(Cut along dotted line
for shoe back)*

THE SULTAN RAG DOLL

The sultan is a ruler from the Middle East, a powerful figure of great wealth who appears in Arabian adventure stories such as Aladdin and Sinbad. His daughter is the Arabian princess.

MATERIALS

- ◆ basic medium rag doll

- ◆ a 500 × 1,144mm (19¾in × 45in) piece of black and gold cotton fabric

- ◆ a 305 × 915mm (12 × 36in) piece of gold and burgundy chiffon (or part of a chiffon scarf)

- ◆ a 125 × 255mm (5 × 10in) piece of black and gold lurex fabric

- ◆ a 150 × 330mm (6 × 13in) piece of maroon-coloured nylon (of the type used in petticoats)

- ◆ a 150mm (6in) square of black felt

- ◆ a small amount of black double knitting yarn

- ◆ an assortment of embroidery silks

- ◆ a length of thin elastic

- ◆ velcro or pop fasteners

Features

Before sewing the rag doll together, you will need to sew the sultan's features onto the front of the head, although the moustache and beard should be added later, at the same time as making the hair. When choosing the colours for the embroidery silks, bear in mind that the olive complexion of the sultan should influence you towards dark colours. The hair will need to be black, which will dictate the colour of the eyebrows and the eye outline; furthermore, the fabric from which the doll is made should be somewhat darker in shade to suit his Middle Eastern skin tone. The colour of the embroidery silk for the eyes is a warm almond brown.

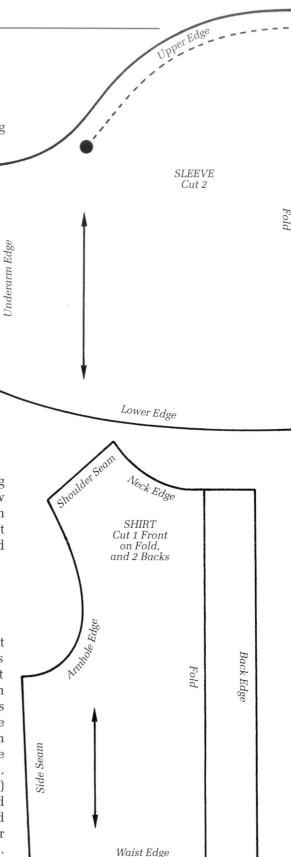

Hair

Cut thirty lengths of 100mm (4in) long black double knitting yarn, fold each strand in half and sew into place at the back of the head by hand, following the neckline.

Moustache

Using a darning needle and a length of black double knitting yarn, sew a line of small stitches from one end of the moustache to the other, and for its centre, wind some more black yarn around a finger four times. Secure together with a few stitches and sew into place at the centre front, trimming to the required length.

The Sultan's features.

Beard

Cut ten length of yarn, each measuring 50mm (2in) long, fold in half and sew into position beneath the mouth to form the rough shape of the beard. Snip it here and there until you are satisfied with the shape.

Shirt

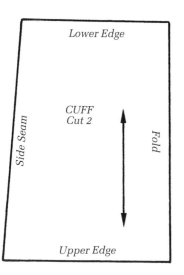

Cut out one shirt front and two shirt backs from the black and gold fabric, as shown on the pattern and, with right sides together, take a 6mm (¼in) seam and sew the front and back pieces together along the shoulder and side seams. Turn a double 6mm (¼in) hem down the back and lower edges of the shirt, which will give it a neat finish. Cut and sew into place a 38mm (1½in) wide bias strip cut from the gold and black fabric sufficiently long to bind the neck edge. Sew pop fasteners or velcro into place along the back edges.

From the black and gold fabric, cut out two sleeve pieces and two sleeve cuffs and then, with right sides together, join the underarm sleeve seams. Next, run a gather stitch along the lower edge of the sleeve and another along the upper sleeve edge between the dots, and sew the sleeve into the shirt, gathering it up to fit the armhole edge. Repeat the same process for the second sleeve. Now place the shirt onto the doll and gather up the lower edge of both sleeves, securing them tightly. Turn and sew a 6mm (¼in) hem on the lower edge of each sleeve cuff; also sew a 6mm (¼in) hem at the top edge of the cuff. Placing the cuff's upper edge onto the sleeve's lower edge, sew neatly into place. Turn a hem at the side seams of the cuff and close the seam at the back of the sleeve cuff by overstitching.

Overstitch the cuff edges together.

Pants

From the remaining black and gold fabric, cut out two pants pieces, making certain to place the pattern piece on the fold of the fabric as indicated on the pattern. With right sides together, sew a 6mm (¼in) seam along the inside leg edge, turn a double 6mm (¼in) hem along the lower edge to form a casing for the elastic and, with right sides together, sew a 6mm (¼in) seam joining the centre front and back seams. Turn over a double 6mm (¼in) hem at the waist edge to form a casing for the elastic. Thread the elastic through the lower leg casings and the waist casings, securing the elastic to the required length.

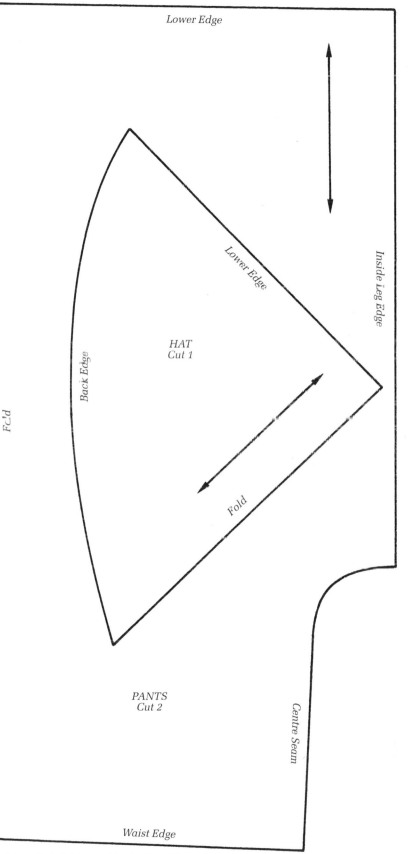

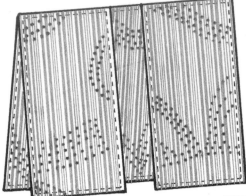

Sew the robe as shown by the dotted lines.

Wind the braiding around the cummerbund.

Place the padded rim over the hat.

Robe

Cut out three rectangles from the burgundy and gold fabric, consisting of two front pieces each measuring 165mm (6½in) wide by 305mm (12in) long, and one back piece measuring 356mm (14in) wide by 305mm (12in) long. Turn a 6mm (¼in) hem all the way around each piece and then, with right sides together, join the front and back pieces along the shoulder seams, leaving a gap at the centre back for the neck, and gather the shoulder seams tightly. To make the cummerbund, you will need a strip of maroon-coloured fabric 38mm (1½in) wide by 178mm (7in) long. With right sides together, sew a seam 6mm (¼in) down one short end and along the length of the cummerbund, trimming seams and snipping corners. Turn the material to the right side and fold a 6mm (¼in) hem at the open end. Slip stitch the edges together. Taking a narrow piece of the gold fabric, or some gold braiding, wind the braid around the cummerbund four times, securing it at the ends and catching it with a few stitches along the back of the cummerbund to keep the braiding in place. Sew a pop fastener, or some velcro, to the cummerbund at the back edges. Gather the robe material at the front and back, and place the cummerbund over the top of the robe around the waist to keep it in position.

Hat

Cut out one hat piece from the black and gold lurex fabric, according to the pattern. With right sides together, sew a 6mm (¼in) seam along the back edge, trim the seam neatly and turn the hat right side out. Stuff it lightly and sew the hat to the head, matching the centre and back dots. Make sure to sew the hat to the hairline at the back of the head. Cut out a piece of maroon-coloured fabric 330mm (13in) long by 90mm (3½in) wide, and a piece of gold and burgundy fabric 380mm (15in) long by 32mm (1¼in) wide. With right sides together, sew a 6mm (¼in) seam along one short edge and along the length of the maroon fabric, then trim the seams and snip the corners. Turn the fabric to the right side and stuff it lightly, then turn a 6mm (¼in) hem at the open end which is secured with a slip stitch. Turn under a 6mm (¼in) hem along the length of the gold fabric, and also along both short ends of the fabric. Secure one end to the back of the maroon fabric. Take the gold fabric and wind it around the padded rim seven times, fastening it to the back of the rim. Sew the two short ends of the maroon-coloured padded rim together to form a doughnut shape, place this over the part of the hat that is already on the doll and sew it into place along the lower hat edge.

Shoes

Cut out four pieces of shoe pattern from the black felt, oversew two pieces together along the curved edge, turn right side out and place onto the doll's foot. Sew the upper edge of the shoe onto the doll's foot, and finish off with a decoration of your choice.

*SHOE
Cut 4*

Accessories

The sultan has a gold chain around his neck and a small sword, which is actually a tiepin obtained at a local Christmas bazaar. However, these items are not suitable for small children.

THE ARABIAN PRINCESS RAG DOLL

The olive-skinned Arabian princess lives a life of great luxury and untold riches in an exotic palace somewhere in the desert.

MATERIALS

- ◆ basic medium rag doll

- ◆ a 203 × 406mm (8 × 16in) piece of purple satin fabric

- ◆ a 255 × 458mm (10 × 18in) piece of patterned chiffon (or part of a chiffon scarf)

- ◆ a 150mm (6in) square of bright pink shantung fabric

- ◆ a 150mm (6in) square of pink cotton fabric

- ◆ a 203 × 150mm (8 × 6in) piece of iron-on interfacing

- ◆ 1m (39⅜in) of wide braid

- ◆ a small amount of black double knitting yarn

- ◆ an assortment of embroidery silks

- ◆ gold lurex thread

- ◆ pearl and braid motifs

- ◆ a short length of thin elastic

- ◆ velcro or pop fasteners

Features

Before you begin to sew the rag doll together, you must transfer the princess's features onto the head of the

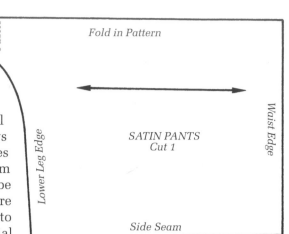

doll in pencil. When selecting the coloured silks for the princess, try to keep in mind that being Arabian should influence you towards dark colours. The hair will need to be black, and this will dictate the colour of her eyebrows and the outline of the eyes. The eyes themselves are sewn from a warm almond brown, which could also be used for the nose, and the lips are embroidered in a deep red to brighten the features. The material used to make the princess is slightly darker than the usual cream-coloured fabric from which the other dolls are made, which should suit the Arabian skin tone.

Hair

Cut a piece of card measuring 305 × 100mm (12 × 4in) to be used as a template, and wind black double knitting yarn around it fifty times. Sew the yarn together along one edge of the card, then

The Princess's features.

Catch the back of the hair at the neck with braiding.

slip the yarn off the template. Using the sewn edge as a parting, sew the yarn into place along the centre line of the head, between the dot at the centre front and the dot at the centre back. The hair will then fall as a long loop down the doll's back. Catch the back of the hair very loosely at the nape of the neck with braiding. Note that the length of the card template determines how long the hair will be.

Satin Pants

Cut out one pants piece from the purple satin fabric, placed on the fold in the fabric as shown in the pattern, and turn a 6mm (¼in) hem around the lower leg edge. With right sides together, sew a 6mm (¼in) seam along the side seams, turn a double 6mm (¼in) hem along the waist edge to form a casing for the elastic, then thread the elastic through and secure it to the required length.

Camisole

From the piece of pink shantung silk, cut out one camisole front and two camisole backs as indicated on the pattern. With right sides of the fabric

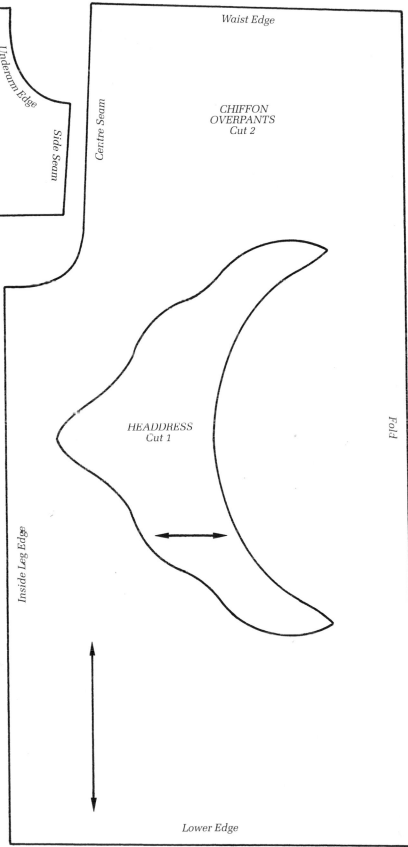

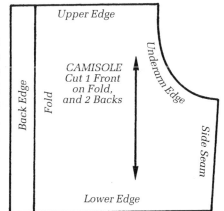

together, sew a 6mm (¼in) seam along the side seam of the camisole. Cut out and sew another camisole top from the cotton fabric to be used as a lining. Then, with right sides together, join the camisole to the lining along all the edges, leaving the lower edge unsewn to permit the camisole to be turned the right way. Trim the seams neatly, snipping the corners to allow the fabric to sit better, and turn the camisole to the right side. Turn a 6mm (¼in) hem along the bottom edges of both camisole and lining, and slip stitch together. Sew two pieces of braiding approximately 50mm (2in) long to the camisole front and back as shoulder straps, and attach pop fasteners or velcro to the back.

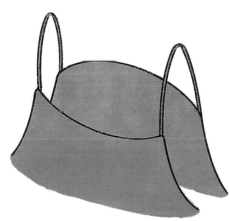

Attach braiding to front and back of the camisole to form straps.

Chiffon Overpants

From your chosen colour of chiffon fabric, cut out two overpants pieces, placing them on the fold of the fabric as stated on the pattern. With right sides together, sew a 6mm (¼in) seam along the inside

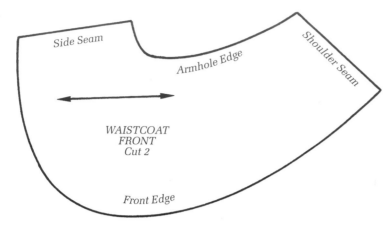

WAISTCOAT
FRONT
Cut 2

Side Seam

Armhole Edge

Shoulder Seam

Front Edge

(*right*) The Princess's sandals.

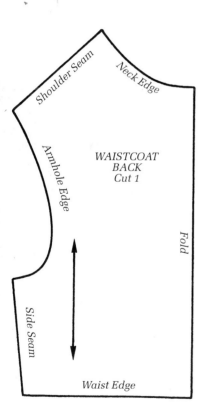

WAISTCOAT
BACK
Cut 1

Shoulder Seam

Neck Edge

Armhole Edge

Side Seam

Fold

Waist Edge

leg edges. Repeat for the other leg. Taking a 6mm (¼in) seam, join the overpants pieces together along the centre seam. Turn a double 6mm (¼in) hem along the lower edge of the pants and waist edge to form a casing for the elastic. Thread a length of elastic through and secure to the required length. Sew braiding around the waist and ankle hems for decoration.

Waistcoat

Cut out a piece of purple satin measuring 203 × 150mm (8 × 6in), and back it with an iron-on interfacing to lessen the amount of fraying and to make the waistcoat appear firmer. Cut out one back waistcoat piece and two front waistcoat pieces as shown on the pattern and, with right sides of the material together, sew a 6mm (¼in) seam along the shoulder and side seams. Trim these neatly, bind all raw outer edges and armhole edges with braiding, folded in half to form a casing.

Accessories

The doll has been given gold braid sandals. These are made by sewing gold lurex thread to the feet to form a sandal pattern, then sewing or gluing a pearl and braid motif to the centre to add decoration.

Arabian princesses would be expected to wear gold jewellery, so the doll has been given a few gold bracelets up her arms and a gold and black dropper attached to the centre parting of her hair. These are optional, and you may have your own ideas about what sort of accessories you would prefer for your doll.

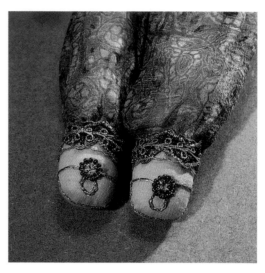

HEADDRESS

Cut out a piece of purple satin measuring 125mm (5in) long and 100mm (4in) wide, backing the fabric with iron-on interfacing to prevent it fraying, then cut out the headdress pattern. Bind the raw edges of the headdress with a braid. Place a pearl and braid motif in the middle of the headdress, and sew it into place on top of the head.

NECKLACE

The necklace is a piece of gold lurex thread onto which has been sewn at its centre a pearl and braid motif, the thread being tied to the back of the neck.

Many of the accessories will need to be altered if your child is thought to be too young for beads and pearls.

THE VICTORIAN BATHER RAG DOLL

In the nineteenth century, when bathing in the sea became very fashionable, the convention of the day meant that men and women used to go into the water fully clothed in elaborate bathing costumes. Our own doll is ready to take a dip in the briny.

MATERIAL

- basic medium doll

- a 500 × 915mm (19¾ × 36in) piece of navy cotton fabric

- 3m (118in) of white satin ribbon 3mm (⅛in) wide

- 1m (39⅜in) of white satin bias binding 13mm (½in) wide

- 1m (39⅜in) of navy binding or ribbon 6mm (¼in) wide

- a small amount of brown double knitting yarn

- an assortment of coloured embroidery silks

- a 150mm (6in) square of black felt

- a short length of thin elastic

- velcro or pop fasteners

Features

Before sewing the rag doll together, you will need to transfer the Victorian bather's features onto the front of the doll's head with a well-sharpened pencil (as shown for the Bride Doll on page 46), When selecting the coloured silks for the bather, it would be best to choose natural colours.

(*right*) The sewn edge forms a centre parting.

Hair

Cut a card template measuring 50mm (2in) wide by 230mm (9in) long, and wind the brown double knitting yarn around it approximately fifty times. Sew the yarn together securely along one edge of the card and snip the yarn at the other end. Find the centre of the hair and open it out flat. Use the line of

sewing as a centre parting to be sewn down the back of the head. Divide each side of the hair into three sections and plait them, securing the ends with a piece of yarn of the same colour. Taking the completed plait, curve it towards the back of the head and fasten it just below the hair in the middle of the head 13mm (½in) or so from the centre back. Complete the other plait in the same way.

To make the clusters of loops for the front of the hair, cut another template, this time measuring 38mm (1½in) wide by 50mm (2in) long, wind the yarn around it ten times, fasten the loops together with a few stitches and attach them to the centre front of the doll just in front of the parting for the plaited hair. Make two more clusters of loops and, when finished, secure them to the front of the doll's head an equal distance apart.

The length of each card template determines how long the plaits and loop clusters will be.

Mob Cap

Cut a circle of 178mm (7in) diameter from the navy-coloured cotton fabric and, taking the piece of white satin bias binding, sew around the mob cap to encase the raw edge. Sew a gathering stitch 13mm (½in) from the cap edge all the way around the circle, pull the gathering stitches together to enable the cap to fit onto the doll's head, and fasten in place.

Bloomers

Cut out two bloomer pieces from the navy-coloured cotton fabric. Turn and sew a double 6mm (¼in) hem along the lower edge of the bloomers, and then sew a length of 3mm (⅛in) wide white satin ribbon 6mm (¼in) from the lower edge. To form a casing for the elastic, sew 6mm (¼in) wide navy binding or ribbon onto the bloomers as shown on the pattern. Thread the elastic through the casing so that it fits around the doll's leg, securing the elastic into place with a few stitches at both ends of the casing. Do the same for the other bloomer piece. With right sides of the fabric together, sew a 6mm (¼in) seam joining inside leg edges. Place right sides facing and join the bloomer pieces together along centre seams, then trim the seams neatly and snip into the curves. Sew a double 6mm (¼in) hem along the waist edge to form a casing for the elastic, thread the elastic through the casing and fasten it to the required length.

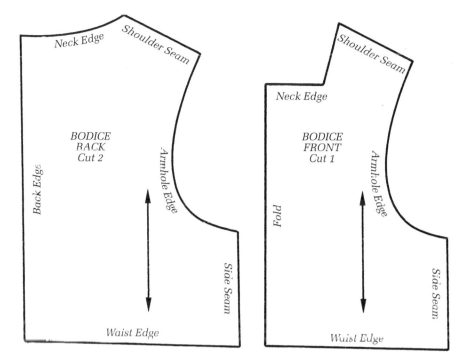

Bodice

Cut out one bodice front and two bodice back pieces, as shown on the pattern. With the right sides together, take a 6mm (¼in) seam and sew the front and back bodice pieces together along the shoulder and side seams, trimming the seams neatly. Cut out and sew another bodice in the same way, to be used as a lining. With the right sides of the fabric together, sew the bodice piece to the lining at the back edge and along the neckline. Trim the seams and clip into the corners and curves. Turn the bodice to the right side and press. Using a tacking stitch, sew the bodice and the lining together at the armhole edges.

Sleeves

Cut out two sleeve pieces as shown on the pattern. Sew a double 6mm (¼in) hem along the lower sleeve edge, and sew a length of 3mm (⅛in) wide white satin ribbon 6mm (¼in) away from the sleeve's lower edge. To form the casing for the elastic, sew a length of navy binding or ribbon onto the sleeve as shown on the pattern. Thread a piece of elastic through the casing to fit the upper arm, and secure the elastic into place with a few small stitches. With right sides of the fabric together, sew a 6mm (¼in) seam joining the underarm edges. Gather along the armhole edge of each sleeve between the dots, as indicated on the pattern. Matching the sleeve seams to the side seams of the bodice, gather the top of the sleeve to fit the armhole, and sew the sleeve into place. Trim the seams neatly and oversew the raw edges.

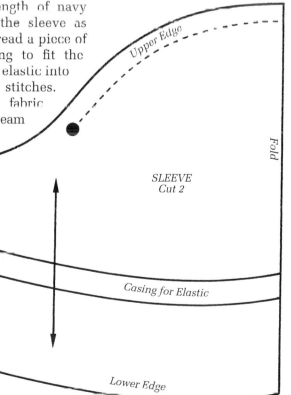

Skirt

Cut out a piece of navy fabric measuring 165 × 560mm (6½ × 22in). Turn a double 13mm (½in) hem along the skirt's lower edge, and sew a 3mm (⅛in) wide white satin ribbon along the hemline 13mm (½in) away from the lower skirt edge. Sew another length of the same ribbon 6mm (¼in) up from the first. With right sides together, sew a 6mm (¼in) seam joining the centre back edges, leaving 50mm (2in) open at the waist edge for the back opening. Neaten the raw edges of the opening. Gather the waist edge of the skirt and sew it to the lower edge of the bodice, taking a 6mm (¼in) seam and, making certain to leave the bodice lining free, trim the seam neatly. Turn under 6mm (¼in) at the lower edge of the bodice lining and slip stitch the waist edge of the bodice lining and skirt together, encasing the waist seam. Sew a 3mm (⅛in) wide white satin ribbon all the way around the neckline 6mm (¼in) away from the neck edge. Sew a piece of 3mm (⅛in) wide white satin ribbon to decorate the waistline. Finally, sew velcro or pop fasteners to the bodice's back opening.

Shoes

Cut out four pieces of shoe pattern from the black felt, oversew two pieces together along the curved edge, turn right side out and place onto the doll's foot, sewing it into position by the upper edge. To decorate the shoe, sew a piece of 3mm (⅛in) wide white satin ribbon around the top, leaving a little of the black felt showing above it.

*SHOE
Cut 4*

THE MEDIEVAL RAG DOLL

Lady Rowena comes from the days of medieval castles with tall round turrets and damsels in distress awaiting a knight in shining armour to come on his white charger to rescue them.

MATERIALS

◆ basic medium rag doll

◆ a 500 × 915mm (19¾ × 36in) piece of pink jersey fabric

◆ a 255 × 203mm (10 × 8in) piece of coarse cream linen or curtain lining

◆ a 230 × 305mm (9 × 12in) piece of pink chiffon

◆ a quantity of yellow double knitting yarn

◆ an assortment of coloured embroidery silks

◆ a 150mm (6in) square of burgundy felt

◆ one pink pipe-cleaner

◆ a quantity of gold lurex thread

◆ a length of pearl trimming

◆ a short length of thin elastic

◆ velcro and pop fasteners

Features

Before sewing the rag doll together, transfer Lady Rowena's features onto the front of the head in pencil (as shown for the Bride Doll on page 46). The silks for

the medieval doll are chosen for their simplicity, with the eyebrows and eye outline embroidered in a caramel brown together with the nose. She has a red mouth, while her eyes are a beautiful blue.

Hair

The hair is made using the yellow double knitting yarn and a card template measuring 100mm (4in) wide by 203mm (8in) long. Wind the yarn around the template approximately 100 times, sew it securely along one edge of the card and snip it at the other end, then open out the yarn flat and use the line of sewing as a parting down the centre, sewing into place. Divide the hair on each side of the head into three equal parts and plait them, securing the ends of the plait with a small length of yarn and curving them to meet at the back of the head. To make the plait for the back of the head use the same card template and wind the yellow double knitting yarn around it thirty-six times. Once again, sew the yarn along one edge of the template and cut it along the other, then take the sewn edge and place it down the centre back below the other hair. Divide the hair into three equal parts, as previously, and plait it together. Secure the plait with a piece of yarn of the same colour, and then twist some of the gold lurex

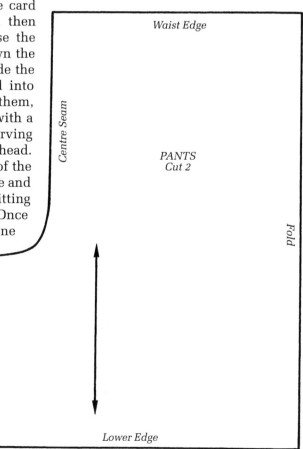

Secure the second section of hair at the back of the head below the first section.

thread around the plait as decoration. The length of the template denotes how long you wish the hair to be.

Pants

Cut out two pants pieces from the coarse cream fabric. With right sides of the fabric facing, sew a 6mm (¼in) seam joining the inside leg edges. Do the same for the other leg piece. Now join the pants pieces together along the centre seams, trimming the seams neatly and snipping into the curves. Hem along the lower edge of the pants pieces. Sew a double 6mm (¼in) hem along the waist edge to form a casing for the elastic, and thread the thin elastic through the casing, securing it to the required length.

Waist Edge

Centre Seam

*PANTS
Cut 2*

Fold

Inside Leg Edge

Lower Edge

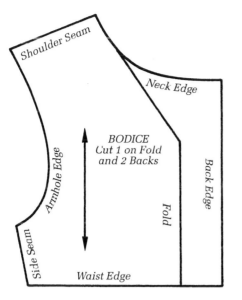

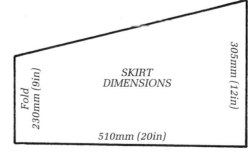

Dress

Cut out one bodice front and two bodice backs from the pink jersey fabric, as shown on the pattern. With right sides together, take a 6mm (¼in) seam and sew the shoulder and side seams, trimming neatly. Cut out and sew another bodice to be used for the lining. With right sides facing, sew the bodice to the lining at the centre back and neck edges. Trim the seams neatly and snip into the corners and curves. Turn the bodice right side out and press. Using a tacking stitch, sew the bodice and lining together at the armhole edges. Decorate the bodice by sewing a length of gold lurex thread around the neckline.

Sleeves

From the pink jersey fabric, cut out two sleeve pieces as shown on the pattern. With right sides together, join the underarm seam. Turn and sew a 6mm (¼in) hem along the lower sleeve edge. Deco-

rate the sleeve edge with a row of gold lurex thread and a tassel. To make the tassel, wind some lurex thread around two fingers to form loops, tie a length of the thread around the top of the loops to secure them together, sew the tassel to the bottom of the sleeve to add weight, ease the sleeve into the bodice armhole and sew it in place.

Skirt

Cut out a skirt piece from the same pink jersey fabric. Sew a double 6mm (¼in) hem along the skirt's lower edge, decorating it with a length of the lurex thread. With right sides of the fabric together, join the back edges of the skirt taking a 6mm (¼in) seam, leaving 75mm (3in) open to form the back opening. Turn a hem at the back opening to neaten. Pleat the waist edge of the skirt to fit into the waist edge of the bodice, making certain to pleat the fabric to face the centre front of the skirt. Sew the waist edge of the skirt to the bodice taking a 6mm (¼in) seam and, leaving the lining free, turn a 6mm (¼in) hem along the waist edge of the bodice lining and slip stitch the lining into place, encasing the waist seam. Sew pop fasteners or velcro to the back opening.

Headdress

The headdress is made from a pink fluffy pipe-cleaner. Twist its ends together to form a circle, bend the pipe cleaner to the required shape, then wind the pearl trimming around it, repeating the process with a length of gold lurex thread and fastening both at

The back of the head-dress.

the back. Cut a piece of chiffon measuring 230mm (9in) long and 305mm (12in) wide, and turn a 6mm (¼in) hem all the way around. Run a line of gathering stitches along one wide edge, and another row 100mm (4in) below. Gather the stitches together and sew the first line of the gathers to the centre front of the head, and a second line down the centre back of the head, covering the ends of the plaits. Place the centre of the pipe-cleaner to the centre front of the head, securing it with a few stitches; now take the back of the pipe-cleaner and secure it to the centre back of the head underneath the hanging veil of the chiffon, which will make the chiffon fabric stand away from the head slightly.

Shoes

Cut out four shoe pieces from the burgundy-coloured felt, oversew two pieces together along the curved edge, turn the shoe pieces to the right side and place them onto the doll's foot. Sew the upper edge of the shoe to the doll. Decorate by sewing a trimming of gold lurex thread around the upper edge of the shoe.

SHOE
Cut 4

Accessory

NECKLACE

The necklace is formed by placing a length of gold lurex thread around the doll's neck and tying it into a knot.

4 The Large Rag Doll

THE BASIC LARGE RAG DOLL

The large rag doll is a little more adventurous in its sewing techniques; it now progresses to arm and leg joints, and feet with sole pieces which permit the doll to stand with both of its feet flat on the floor. This doll will become a favourite with children of all ages, as it looks more like the original rag doll. It is also the right size to dress in 12 to 18 month baby clothes, so you could keep any of the beautiful clothes that are nowadays available for small children, and let them use those to dress their rag doll as they want to.

As with all of the other dolls in this book, each doll's face is embroidered by hand to give it added charm and character.

MATERIALS

- ◆ a piece of cream-coloured cotton fabric measuring 1,144 × 500mm (45 × 19¾in) from which all pattern pieces are cut

- ◆ a quantity of stuffing

- ◆ heavy-duty card

- ◆ a selection of different coloured embroidery silks for the doll's face

- ◆ tracing paper

Making the Doll

Trace all of the relevant pattern pieces from the book onto tracing paper, making sure to transfer all the markings where indicated. You will find that some of the patterns in the book have had to be split up in order to fit them onto a page. The pattern pieces will show exactly where they should be joined together by the letters A and B.

Place all of the pattern pieces onto the cotton material, making sure to line up the arrows indicated on the pattern pieces to the selvedge of the material. Before removing each pattern piece from the material, mark any darts that may be required, or dots such as those that show where the head gusset joins the head front and back pieces. Place the cut-out front head piece on top of the doll's face and trace the features onto the fabric with a well-sharpened pencil. You are now ready to commence sewing the rag doll pieces together. Taking a 6mm (¼in) seam, sew the head gusset to the front of the head, matching

Join the pattern pieces at A and B.

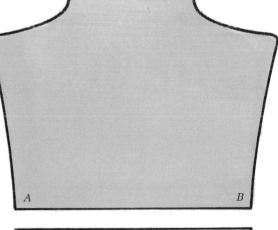

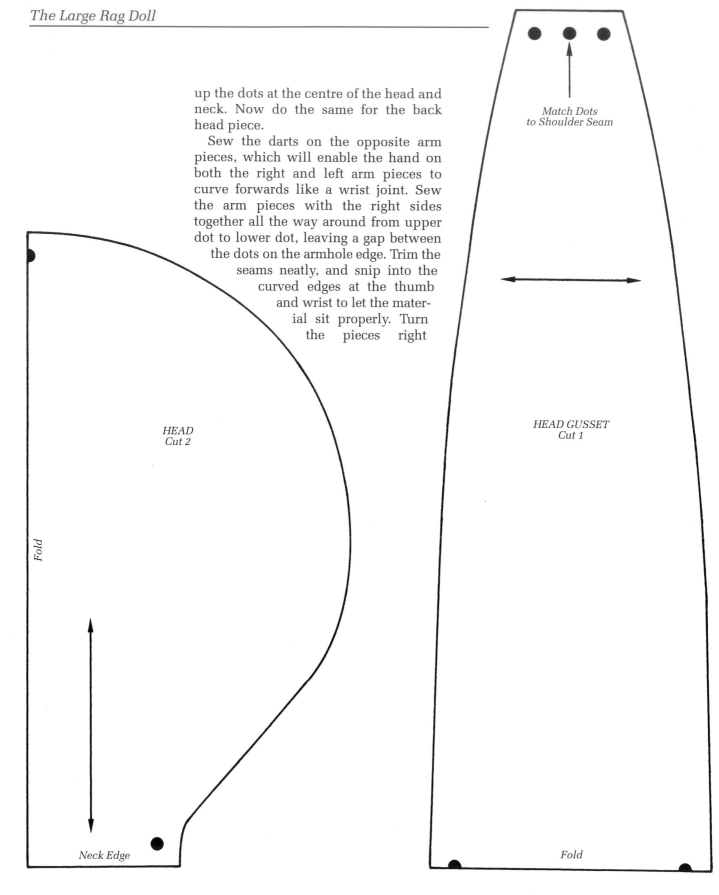

*Match Dots
to Shoulder Seam*

up the dots at the centre of the head and neck. Now do the same for the back head piece.

Sew the darts on the opposite arm pieces, which will enable the hand on both the right and left arm pieces to curve forwards like a wrist joint. Sew the arm pieces with the right sides together all the way around from upper dot to lower dot, leaving a gap between the dots on the armhole edge. Trim the seams neatly, and snip into the curved edges at the thumb and wrist to let the material sit properly. Turn the pieces right

Fold

*HEAD
Cut 2*

Neck Edge

*HEAD GUSSET
Cut 1*

Fold

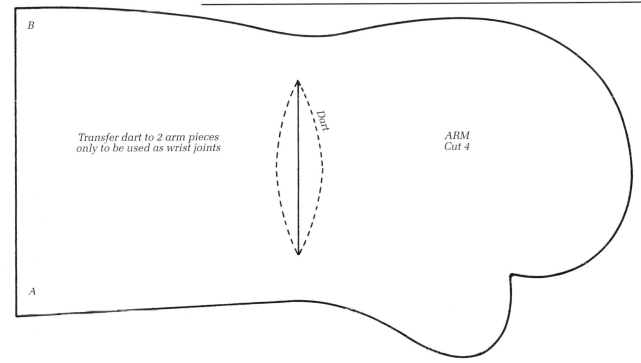

B

*Transfer dart to 2 arm pieces
only to be used as wrist joints*

Dart

ARM
Cut 4

A

sides out and stuff firmly to within
32mm (1¼in) of the armhole edge, and
close the seam with a tacking stitch.

Taking a 6mm (¼in) seam, join the
centre front and centre back seams of
the leg pieces. Trim the seam neatly,
and snip into the front seams at the
ankle curve. Matching the dot on the
sole piece to the front and back seams of
the leg pieces, sew a 6mm (¼in) seam

32mm (1¼in) of the upper leg, closing this
with a tacking stitch.

Sew the shoulder seams on the body
pattern. This will now leave a hole into
which the head will be sewn. Matching
the dots on the head gusset to the

Sew the dart to make a wrist joint.

around the base of the foot, joining the leg
to the sole. Trim the seam neatly, and turn
the leg to the right side. Cut a sole piece
out of the heavy-duty card, making sure
that you follow the inside pattern piece
from the book, and place it inside the finished foot. Stuff the leg firmly to within

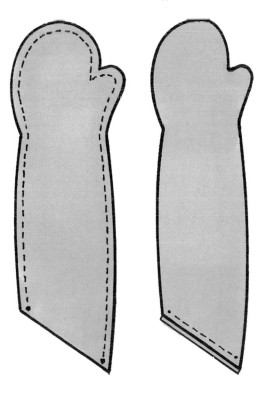

(*far left*) Sew arm pieces
together as shown by the
dotted line.

(*left*) Stitch between the dots
to close the armhole edge.

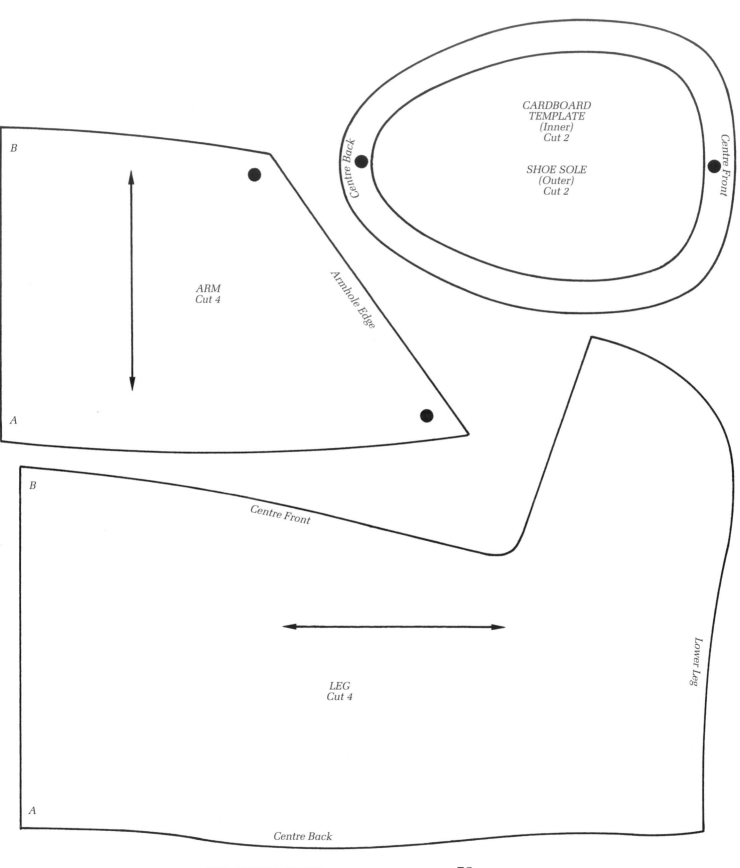

B

ARM
Cut 4

Armhole Edge

Centre Back

Centre Front

CARDBOARD
TEMPLATE
(Inner)
Cut 2

SHOE SOLE
(Outer)
Cut 2

A

B

Centre Front

Lower Leg

LEG
Cut 4

A

Centre Back

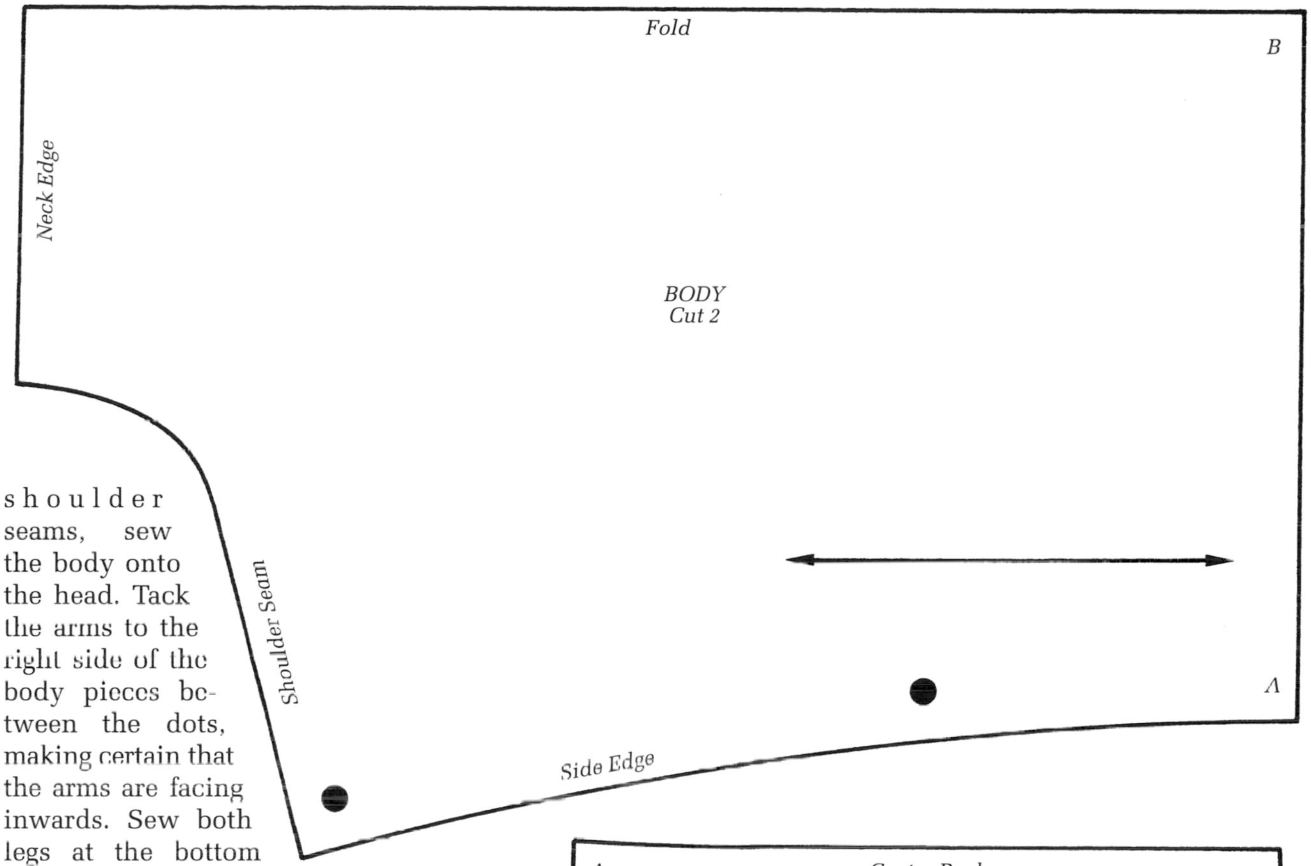

Fold

B

Neck Edge

BODY
Cut 2

Shoulder Seam

Side Edge

A

shoulder seams, sew the body onto the head. Tack the arms to the right side of the body pieces between the dots, making certain that the arms are facing inwards. Sew both legs at the bottom of the body pattern, matching the dots and ensuring that the legs are both facing the right way.

Sew the body pieces right sides together following the side seams; place the arms crossed over inside the body pieces. Turn the doll to the right side, and begin to stuff the head, making sure that the neck is as firm as possible. Continue stuffing the remainder of the body until you are satisfied with the finished result. Sew the bottom of the body pieces together with ladder stitch. The doll is now complete and ready to be dressed.

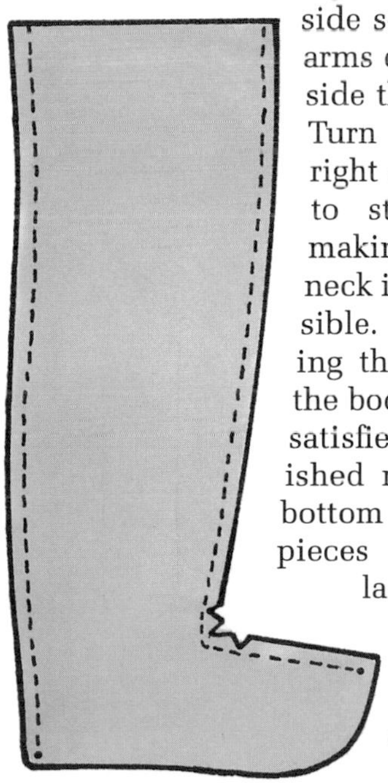

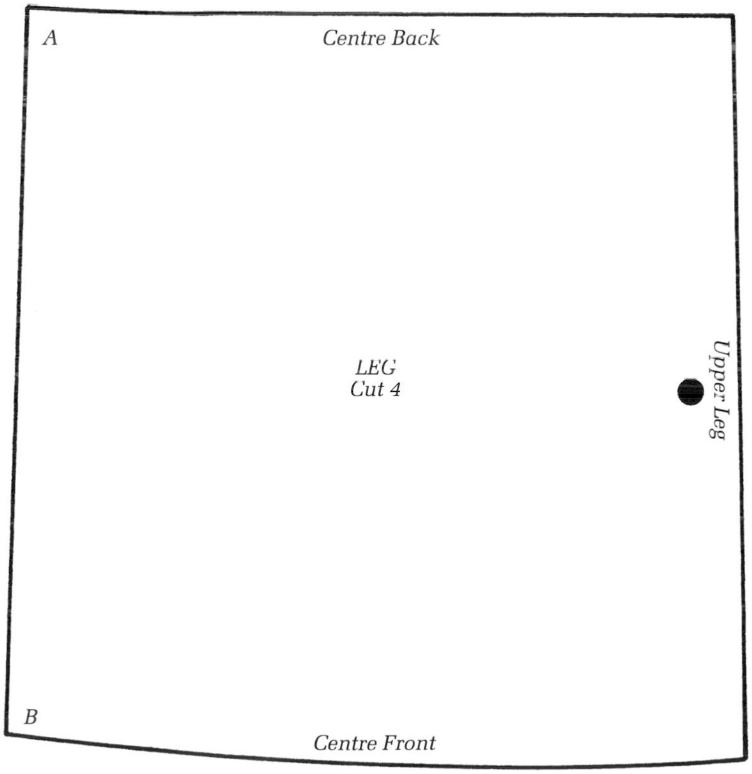

A

Centre Back

LEG
Cut 4

Upper Leg

B

Centre Front

(*left*) Cut notches at the ankle curve.

(*right*) Matching the dots on the head gusset to the shoulder seams, sew the body onto the head.

(*far right*) Join the arms to the body piece, making sure that they are facing the right way round.

(*below right*) Join the legs to the body pieces, making sure that they are facing the right way round.

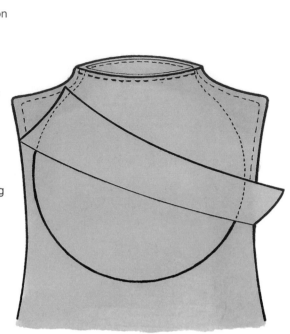

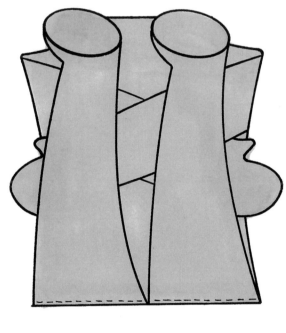

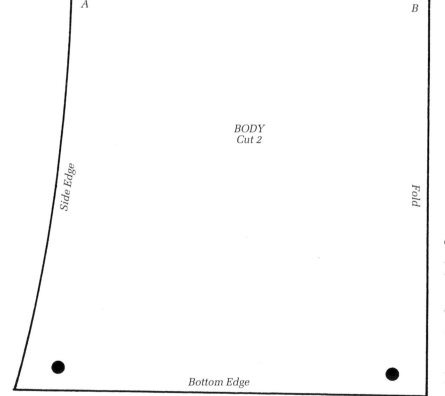

A   B

Side Edge

BODY
Cut 2

Fold

Bottom Edge

THE TRADITIONAL RAG DOLL

The traditional rag doll is different from all of the other dolls in the book, for she does not imitate any particular character or figure, but is simply herself, dressed how you might imagine a typical rag doll should look.

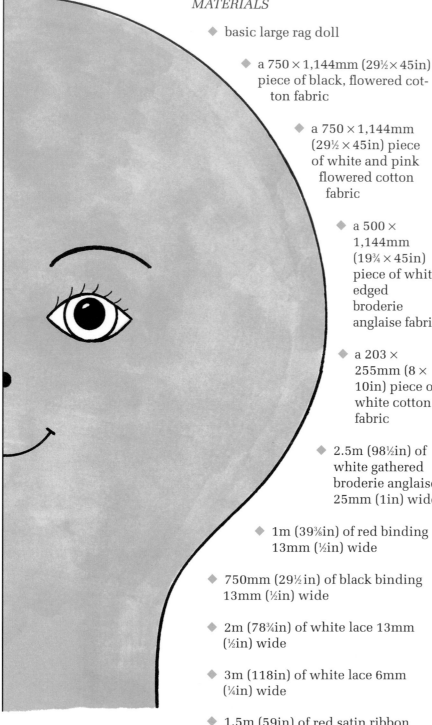

The Traditional Doll's features.

MATERIALS

◆ basic large rag doll

◆ a 750 × 1,144mm (29½ × 45in) piece of black, flowered cotton fabric

◆ a 750 × 1,144mm (29½ × 45in) piece of white and pink flowered cotton fabric

◆ a 500 × 1,144mm (19¾ × 45in) piece of white edged broderie anglaise fabric

◆ a 203 × 255mm (8 × 10in) piece of white cotton fabric

◆ 2.5m (98½in) of white gathered broderie anglaise 25mm (1in) wide

◆ 1m (39⅜in) of red binding 13mm (½in) wide

◆ 750mm (29½in) of black binding 13mm (½in) wide

◆ 2m (78¾in) of white lace 13mm (½in) wide

◆ 3m (118in) of white lace 6mm (¼in) wide

◆ 1.5m (59in) of red satin ribbon 6mm (¼in) wide

◆ 1m (39⅜in) of red narrow satin ribbon 3mm (⅛in) wide

◆ 1m (39⅜in) of elastic 6mm (¼in) wide

◆ 150g of dark brown double knitting yarn

◆ an assortment of embroidery silks

◆ a 305 × 406mm (12 × 16in) piece of black felt

◆ a 305mm (12in) square of red cotton fabric or red felt

◆ two gold-coloured buttons

◆ velcro or pop fasteners

Features

Before sewing the rag doll together, transfer the traditional doll's features onto the front of the head in pencil. When selecting the colours of the silks, the hair colour will indicate the silk needed for the eyebrows and eye outline. Dark brown is used for the hair of the illustrated doll, with a caramel colour for the nose, red for the mouth and a beautiful blue for the eyes.

Hair

Begin by making a fringe, for which you will need to cut a card template measuring 125mm (5in) wide by 75mm (3in) long. Wind the brown double knitting yarn around the template seventy times, sew the yarn together along one edge and snip it along the other edge. Fasten the sewn edge to the centre front of the doll's head. The remaining hair is made from a second template measuring

203mm (8in) wide by 368mm (14⅜in) long, winding the yarn around it approximately 150 times. Once again, sew the yarn along the one edge and cut it at the other, then open the hair out flat and use the sewing line as a parting along the centre back of the head. Sew the hair into place. Now divide the yarn into three equal sections and plait the hair together, repeating the same procedure for the other side. Secure the plaits with a piece of yarn the same colour as the hair. Decorate by tying a piece of red satin ribbon around each plait in the form of a bow.

The length of each template determines the length of the fringe and the main part of the hair.

Pants

From the white and pink cotton fabric, cut out two pants pieces as shown on the pattern. Turn a double 6mm (¼in) hem along the lower edge of the pants pieces to neaten them. Sew a double row of 6mm (¼in) wide white lace, spaced 6mm (¼in) apart along the lower edge of the hemline. With right sides of fabric facing, sew a 6mm (¼in) seam joining the inside leg edges, and then do the same for the other pants piece. Join the pants pieces together taking a 6mm (¼in) seam along the centre seams. Trim neatly and snip into the curves, thereby allowing the seam to sit properly. Turn a double 6mm (¼in) hem along the waist edge to form a casing for the elastic; thread the elastic through the casing and fasten it to the required length. For decoration, cut four lengths of 6mm (¼in) wide red satin ribbon, each measuring 100mm (4in) long, sew one length of ribbon to each dot on the lower outside edge of the pants as indicated on the pattern, and tie the lengths of ribbon in a bow on either leg; this

Box pleat at the side of the pants.

will pull in the material of the pants, forming a box pleat.

Petticoat

Cut out one bodice front and two bodice backs from the white and pink cotton fabric. With right sides of fabric facing, take a 6mm (¼in) seam and sew the front and back bodice pieces together along the side and shoulder seams. Trim the seams neatly. From the piece of white cotton fabric, cut out and sew another bodice in the same way to be used as the bodice lining. With right sides of fabric together, sew the bodice pieces to the lining along the back and neck edges. Trim the seams and cut into the corners and curves. Turn the bodice to the right side and press. Turn over a 6mm (¼in)

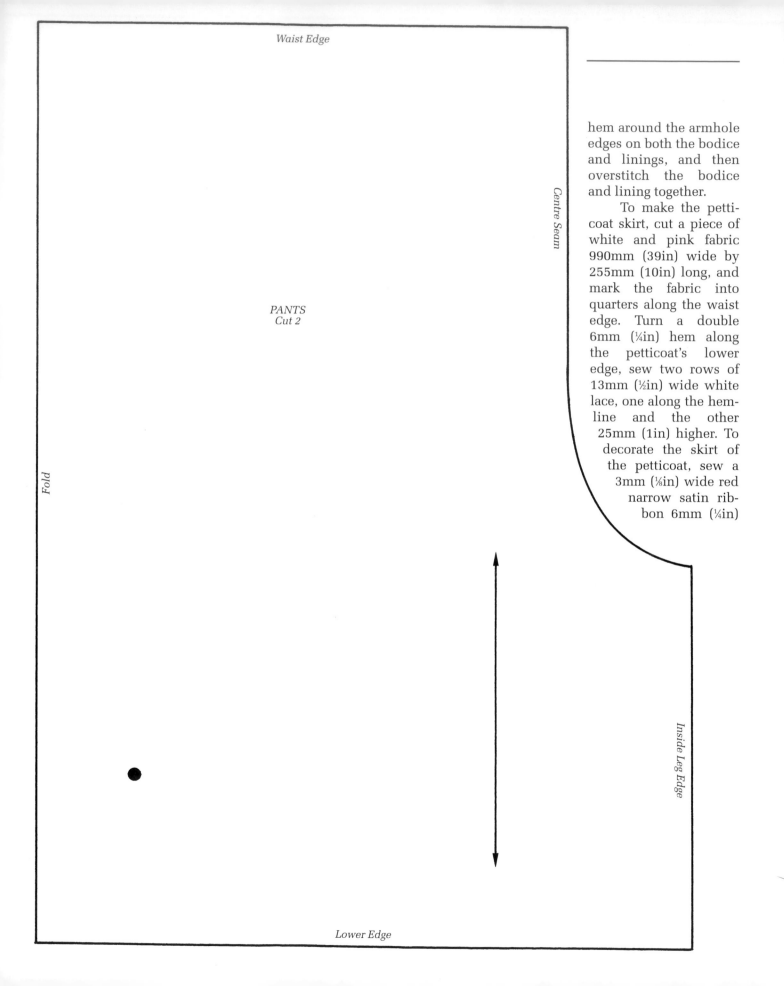

Waist Edge

Centre Seam

PANTS
Cut 2

Fold

Inside Leg Edge

Lower Edge

hem around the armhole edges on both the bodice and linings, and then overstitch the bodice and lining together.

To make the petticoat skirt, cut a piece of white and pink fabric 990mm (39in) wide by 255mm (10in) long, and mark the fabric into quarters along the waist edge. Turn a double 6mm (¼in) hem along the petticoat's lower edge, sew two rows of 13mm (½in) wide white lace, one along the hemline and the other 25mm (1in) higher. To decorate the skirt of the petticoat, sew a 3mm (⅛in) wide red narrow satin ribbon 6mm (¼in)

wide white lace around the neck and armhole edges. Make and sew a red satin bow to decorate the centre of the bodice.

Dress

From the black, flowered fabric, cut out one bodice front and two bodice backs, as shown on the pattern; with right sides together, take a 6mm (¼in) seam and sew the front and back bodice pieces together along the shoulder and side seams, trimming neatly. Turn a double 6mm (¼in) hem down the back of the bodice opening to neaten. Cut a piece of the black flowered fabric on the bias measuring 38mm (1½in) wide by 305mm (12in) long and, with right sides of fabric facing, sew one edge of the bias strip along the neck edge. Turn a hem to neaten the raw edges along the short edges of the bias strip.

above the second row of lace. With right sides of fabric facing, take a 13mm (½in) seam along the back edge of the petticoat, leaving a 75mm (3in) opening at the waist edge, and take a double 6mm (¼in) hem at the back to neaten. Gather the waist edge of the petticoat skirt and match up the quarter division marks on the skirt with the appropriate bodice markings, such as the bodice back, side seams and centre front. Taking a 6mm (¼in) seam, sew the skirt and bodice together, making sure to leave the lining free, then turn under a 6mm (¼in) hem at the waist edge of the bodice lining and slip stitch the lining to the waist seam to finish off. Decorate the bodice of the petticoat by sewing lengths of 6mm (¼in)

Side Seam

Armhole Edge

Shoulder Seam

Neck Edge

Neck Edge

Waist Edge

PETTICOAT BODICE
Cut 1 on Fold for Front and 2 Backs
(cut another set for lining)

Fold

Back Edge

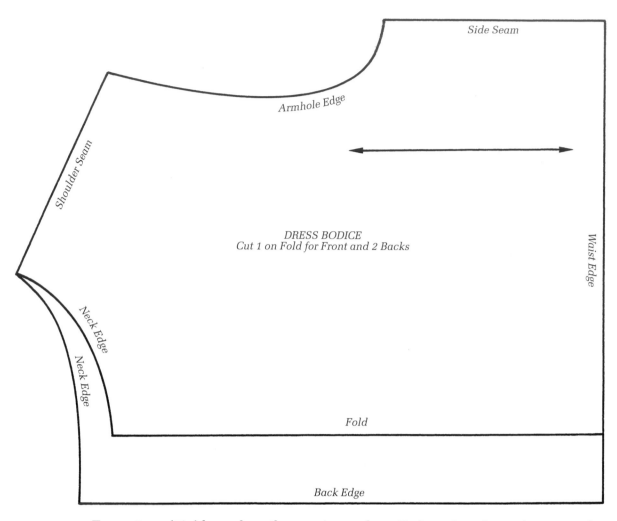

Turn a 6mm (¼in) hem along the remaining long edge of the bias strip and slip stitch it into place, enclosing the seam along the neck edge. Taking the black, flowered fabric, cut out two sleeve pieces, turn a double 6mm (¼in) hem along the sleeve's lower edge, then decorate the sleeve edge by sewing a strip of 25mm (1in) wide gathered broderie anglaise around the inside of the sleeve hemline. Sew a black binding strip onto the back of the sleeve along the line indicated on the pattern to make a casing, then thread a 125mm (5in) length of 6mm (¼in) wide elastic through the casing and secure it at each end of the sleeve edge with a few stitches. Placing the right sides of the fabric together, sew a 6mm (¼in) seam along the underarm edge. Gather the sleeve between the dots and ease it into the armhole, matching the bodice side seams with the sleeve seams, then sew it into place and oversew the raw edges.

To make the dress skirt, cut a piece of black, patterned fabric measuring 990mm (39in) wide by 305mm (12in) long, and mark the fabric into quarters in order to line it up with the bodice later. Turn a double 13mm (½in) hem along the skirt's lower edge. To decorate, sew a strip of 13mm (½in) wide red binding 50mm (2in) above the hemline. With right sides of fabric together, sew a 13mm (½in) seam along the centre back edges, leaving a 75mm (3in) opening at the waist edge. Turn a double 6mm (¼in) hem to neaten the back opening. Gather the

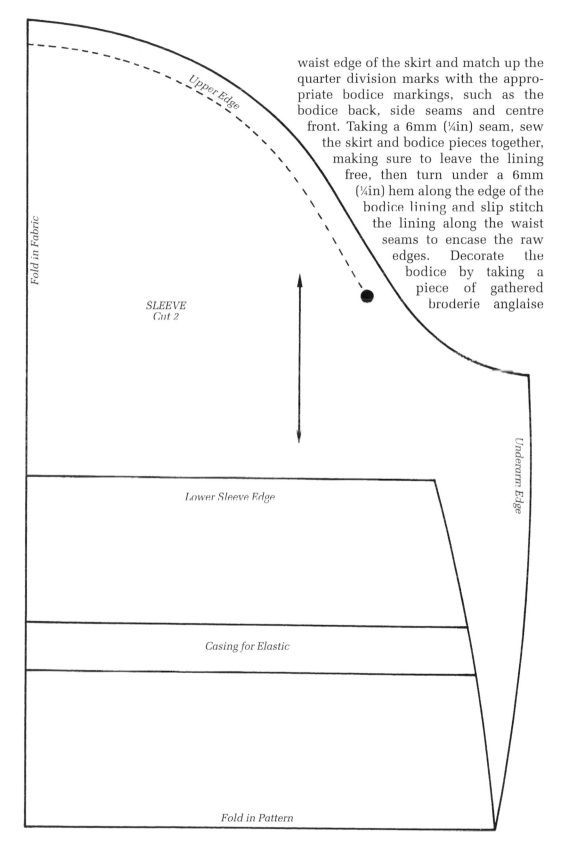

waist edge of the skirt and match up the quarter division marks with the appropriate bodice markings, such as the bodice back, side seams and centre front. Taking a 6mm (¼in) seam, sew the skirt and bodice pieces together, making sure to leave the lining free, then turn under a 6mm (¼in) hem along the edge of the bodice lining and slip stitch the lining along the waist seams to encase the raw edges. Decorate the bodice by taking a piece of gathered broderie anglaise measuring 25mm (1in) wide along the outer neckline and another row along the bias neck edge on the inside, and make and sew a red satin bow to the centre of the bias neck edge. Fasten the back of the bodice by using velcro or pop fasteners.

all the way around the mob cap, pull the gathers up to fit the cap around the doll's head, secure the mob cap into place at the centre front and back, and then make and sew a red satin bow for the front of the cap as decoration.

Apron

From the scalloped edge of the broderie anglaise fabric, cut a piece measuring 203mm (8in) long by 406mm (16in) wide, and a long strip measuring 1,016mm (40in) long and 63mm (2½in) wide which will be used for the ties. Taking the scalloped piece of fabric, neaten the shorter edges by turning a double 6mm (¼in) hem, and gather the waist edge of the apron piece. Find the centre 150mm (6in) of the piece of fabric cut for the ties, and sew the gathered edge of the apron to the tie, fold the tie lengthways and sew a 6mm (¼in) seam on the wrong side, turning the tie the right side out. Do the same for the other side, and slip stitch the centre tie to the waist seam.

Slip-stitch the tie to the apron edge to neaten.

Mob Cap

Cut out a circle from the broderie anglaise fabric measuring 368mm (14⅜in) in diameter, sew a 25mm (1in) wide gathered broderie anglaise strip all the way around the edge of the circle, oversew the edges and iron the seam so that it sits flatter. Sew a gathering stitch 38mm (1½in) in from the scalloped edge

(*right*) The complete shoe.

Shoes

Taking the black felt, cut out two shoe pieces and two shoe soles, then cut out two more shoe pieces from the red cotton fabric, all of which will make both shoes. With right sides of the fabric facing, place the red cotton shoe piece on top of the black felt piece and sew the shoe pieces together along the centre fronts and along the upper shoe edge (as for Little Miss Muffet, *see* page 91). Trim the seams neatly, snipping into the corners and curves, then turn the shoe to the right side and press. Place both thicknesses of the lower shoe piece to the sole and sew into place, which will join the upper shoe to the sole; slip stitch the centre front of the shoe for 25mm (1in), turn the shoe to the right side, turn over the top of the shoe and secure the front with a gold-coloured button.

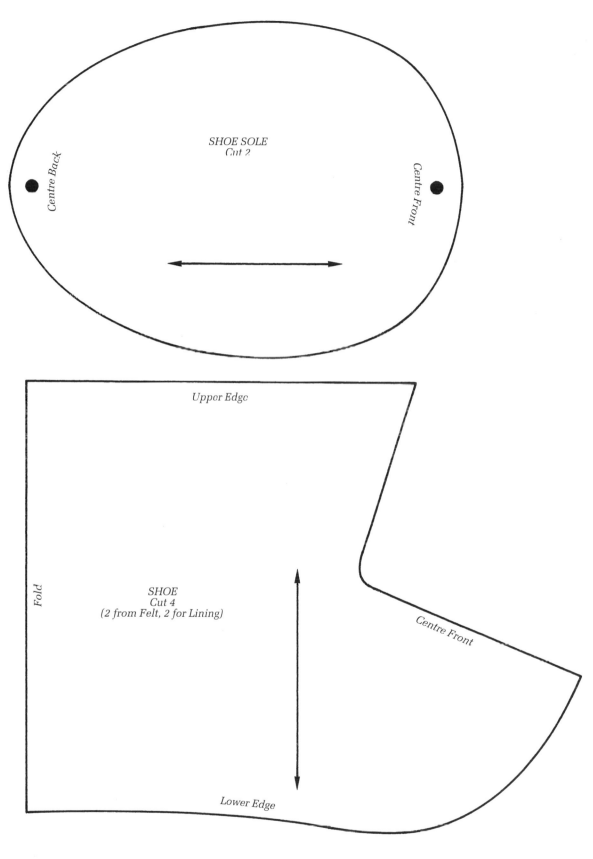

SHOE SOLE
Cut 2

Centre Back

Centre Front

Upper Edge

Fold

SHOE
Cut 4
(2 from Felt, 2 for Lining)

Centre Front

Lower Edge

THE LITTLE MISS MUFFET RAG DOLL

There are many nursery rhyme characters to choose from, but Little Miss Muffet is a constant favourite because, like her, children are usually afraid of spiders – even cheeky spiders with big eyes and fluffy hair.

MATERIALS

- basic large rag doll
- a 1,000 × 1,144mm (39⅜ × 45in) piece of blue spotted cotton fabric
- a 750mm × 1,144mm (29½ × 45in) piece of blue cotton fabric
- a 2.5m (98½in) long by 50mm (2in) wide piece of broderie anglaise lace
- a 500mm (19¾in) long by 25mm (1in) wide piece of gathered broderie anglaise lace
- 1m (39⅜in) of blue satin ribbon 22mm (⅞in) wide
- 500mm (19¾in) of blue satin feather-edged ribbon 13mm (½in) wide
- 3½m (137¾in) of white lace 13mm (½in) wide
- 2m (78¾in) of blue bias binding 13mm (½in) wide
- 2m (78¾in) of blue satin feather-edged ribbon 6mm (¼in) wide
- 2m (78¾in) of blue satin ribbon 6mm (¼in) wide
- 150g of cream double knitting yarn
- an assortment of coloured embroidery silks
- a 305 × 456mm (12 × 16in) piece of white or blue felt
- 1½m (59in) of elastic 6mm (¼in) wide
- one blue flower motif
- velcro or pop fasteners

Features

Before sewing the rag doll together, you will need to transfer Little Miss Muffet's features onto the front of the head (as shown for the Traditional Doll on page 76). When selecting the colours of the silks, bear in mind that the doll is fair. Keep the colours to a natural child shade: the eyebrows, eye outline and nose are embroidered in a soft beige, the mouth in a pastel pink and the eyes a startling blue.

Hair

To make the fringe, cut a card template measuring 125mm (5in) wide by 75mm (3in) long and wind the yarn around the template approximately seventy times. Sew the yarn together securely along one edge of the card and snip it at the other end. Take the sewn edge of the hair and sew it into place along the front seam of the head. Now make a second template, this time measuring 255mm (10in) wide by 280mm (11in) long, and wind the yarn around it 150 times. Sew the yarn firmly together along one edge, as previously, and cut at the other. Place the sewn edge of the hair to the back of the doll's head 100mm (4in) from the centre top of the head.

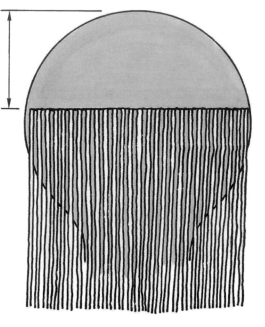

100mm (4in)

(*right*) First row of hair sewn along the back of the head.

(*far right*) The completed pants.

For the remaining hair, cut a third template measuring 114mm (4½in) wide by 356mm (14in) long, and wind the yarn around it 100 times, sewing and snipping as before. Take the sewn edge of the hair and sew it into place at the front seam of the head just behind the fringe. On each side of the centre front, gather together thirty-six strands of hair and secure them with a length of matching yarn to form the doll's bunches. To decorate, take two pieces of 22mm (⅞in) wide blue satin ribbon, each measuring 458mm (18in) long, and tie them to form a bow.

The length of each template denotes how long you wish the hair to be.

Pants

Cut out two pants pieces, as shown on the pattern, from the blue cotton fabric. Turn and sew a double 6mm (¼in) hem along the lower edge of the pants pieces. Decorate the hemline with a row of 13mm (½in) wide white lace. To form a casing for the elastic, sew a length of

blue bias binding to the back of the pants pieces as indicated on the pattern. Thread a 178mm (7in) piece of 6mm (¼in) wide elastic through the casing and secure it into place at both ends with a few small stitches. With right sides of the fabric facing, sew a 6mm (¼in) seam to join the inside leg edges, and do the same for the other pants piece. Join the pants pieces together, taking a 6mm (¼in) seam along the centre seams. Trim

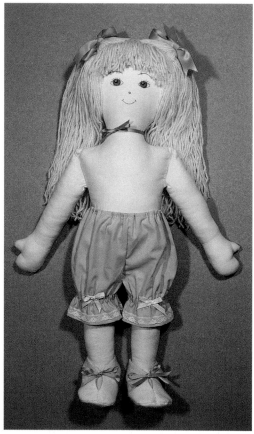

the seams neatly and snip into the curves. Turn a double 6mm (¼in) hem along the waist edge to form a casing for the elastic, then thread the elastic through the casing and fasten it to the required length. To decorate the pants, make and sew a white satin bow to the front of each leg piece.

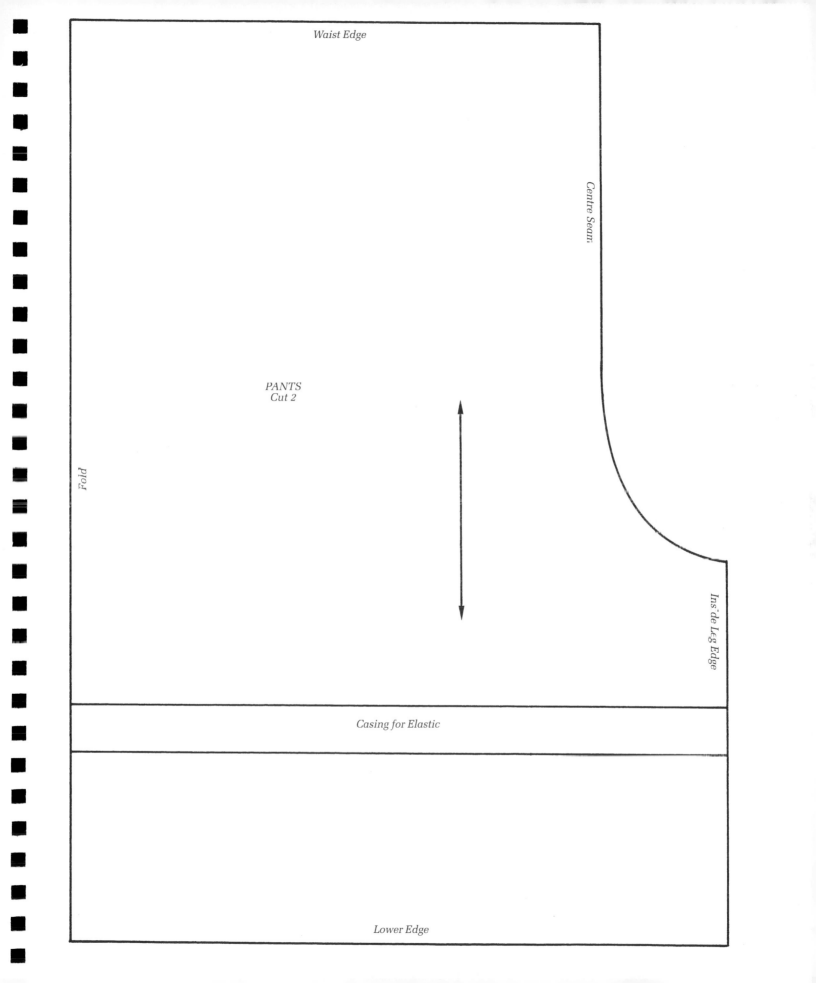

Waist Edge

Centre Seam

PANTS
Cut 2

Fold

Ins de Leg Edge

Casing for Elastic

Lower Edge

Petticoat

From the blue cotton fabric, cut out two bodice fronts and four bodice backs, one set to be used as a lining. With the right sides of the fabric facing, take a 6mm (¼in) seam and sew the front and back bodice pieces together along the side and shoulder seams. Trim the seams neatly, and then repeat the procedure to make the lining. Taking the bodice and lining, place them right sides together and sew a 6mm (¼in) seam along the back and neck edges. Trim the seams and snip into the corners and curves. Turn the bodice to the right side and press. Sew the bodice and lining armholes together and bind the raw edges with a length of the blue bias binding.

To make the petticoat skirt, cut a piece of blue cotton fabric 990mm (39in) wide by 255mm (10in) long, and mark the fabric into quarters along the waist edge. Turn a double 6mm (¼in) hem along the

petticoat's lower edge. For decoration, sew a length of 6mm (¼in) wide blue satin ribbon 25mm (1in) above the petticoat hemline, then, taking the 13mm (¼in) wide white lace, sew two rows back to back on either side of the ribbon. With right sides of fabric together, take a 13mm (½in) seam along the back edge of the petticoat, leaving a 75mm (3in) opening at the waist edge. Sew a double 6mm (¼in) hem at the back opening to neaten. Gather the waist edge of the petticoat and match up the quarter division marks on the skirt with the appropriate bodice marking, such as the bodice back, side seams and centre front. Taking a 6mm (¼in) seam, sew the petticoat skirt and bodice together, making sure to leave the bodice lining free. Turn under a 6mm (¼in) hem at the waist edge of the bodice lining and slip stitch the lining to the waist seam to finish off. Decorate the bodice of the petticoat by sewing a length of 6mm (¼in) wide white lace around the neckline, place a blue flowered motif on the centre front of the bodice and complete the waist edge with a length of 13mm (½in) wide white lace. Secure the back opening with either velcro or pop fasteners.

Dress

Cut out one bodice front and two bodice backs from the blue spotted fabric and another set from the blue cotton fabric to be used as a lining. With the right sides of the bodice pieces together, take a 6mm (¼in) seam and sew the front and back pieces together along the side and shoulder seams, trimming the seams for neatness. Join the lining in the same way. With the right sides of the bodice and the lining facing, join together at the back edge and along the neckline. Trim the seams and clip into the corners and curves. Turn the bodice to the right side and press.

The completed petticoat.

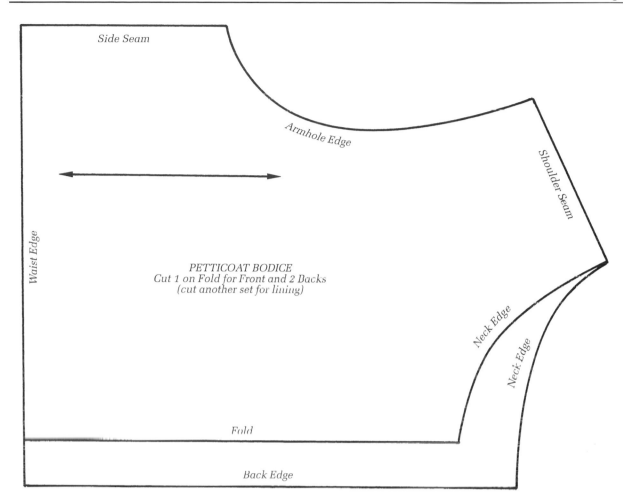

Side Seam

Armhole Edge

Shoulder Seam

Waist Edge

PETTICOAT BODICE
*Cut 1 on Fold for Front and 2 Backs
(cut another set for lining)*

Neck Edge

Neck Edge

Fold

Back Edge

Cut out two sleeve pieces from the blue spotted fabric, turn a double 6mm (¼in) hem along the sleeve's lower edge, and decorate the sleeve by sewing a length of broderie anglaise 50mm (2in) wide along the sleeve edge, covering the top of the broderie anglaise with a strip of 6mm (¼in) wide blue feather-edged ribbon. To make a casing for the elastic, sew a blue binding strip onto the back of the sleeve along the line indicated on the pattern. Thread a 125mm (5in) length of 6mm (¼in) wide elastic through the casing and secure it at each end of the sleeve edge with a few stitches. Placing the right sides of the sleeve together, sew a 6mm (¼in) seam to join the underarm edges. Gather the sleeve between the dots and ease it into the bodice armhole, matching the bodice seams with the sleeve seams. Sew into place, leaving the lining free, turn a 6mm (¼in) hem on the lining armhole and slip stitch into place, encasing the sleeve and armhole raw

The feather-edged ribbon.

edges. Decorate the bodice by sewing a length of 25mm (1in) wide gathered broderie anglaise along the neck edge.

To make the skirt, cut a piece of blue spotted cotton fabric measuring 990mm (39in) wide by 305mm (12in) long, and mark the fabric into quarters to line up with the bodice later. Turn a double 13mm (½in) hem along the skirt's lower edge. To decorate, sew a length of 50mm (2in) wide broderie anglaise along the hemline, placing the top

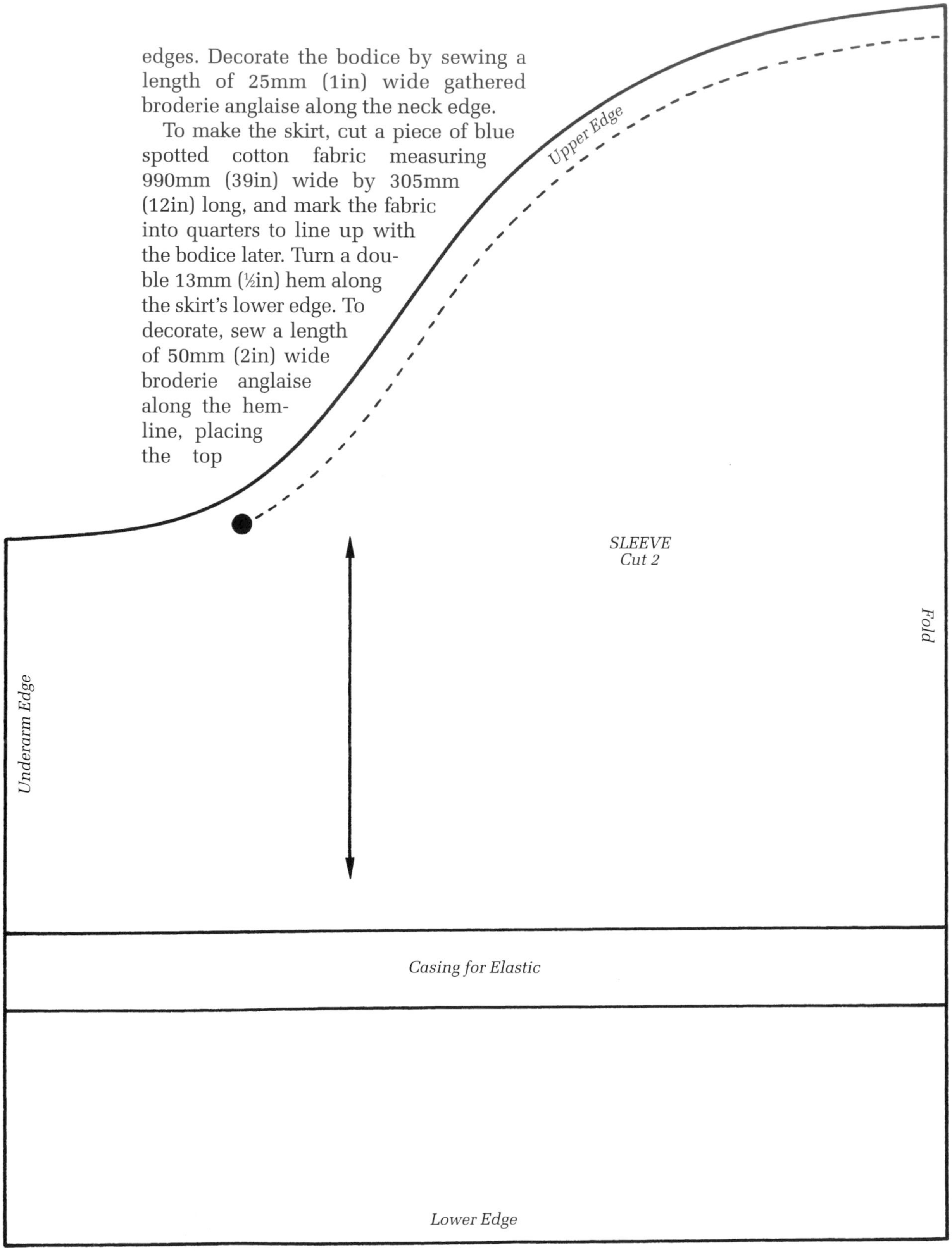

Upper Edge

SLEEVE
Cut 2

Fold

Underarm Edge

Casing for Elastic

Lower Edge

of the broderie anglaise 90mm (3½in) above the hem edge, and sew a length of 6mm (¼in) wide blue satin feather-edged ribbon along it to cover the sewing line. Placing right sides of fabric together, sew a 13mm (½in) seam along the centre back edges, leaving a 75mm (3in) opening at the waist edge. Turn a double 6mm (¼in) hem to neaten the back opening. Gather the waist edge of the skirt, matching up the quarter divisions made on the skirt with the appropriate bodice markings, such as the bodice back, side seams and centre front. Taking a 6mm (¼in) seam, sew the skirt and bodice pieces together, making certain to leave the lining free. Turn under a 6mm (¼in) hem along the waist edge of the bodice lining, and slip stitch the lining along the waist edge to encase the raw edges. Decorate the waistline by sewing a length of 50mm (2in) wide broderie anglaise around the bodice, matching up the scalloped edge of the broderie anglaise with the waist seam. To neaten the top of the broderie anglaise, cover the raw edges with a length of 13mm (½in) wide blue feather-edged satin ribbon and sew into place. Fasten the back of the bodice with velcro or pop fasteners.

Shoes

Cut out two shoe pieces and two shoe soles from the white or blue felt; also cut out two shoe pieces from the blue spotted fabric. Altogether, this will make both shoes. With the right sides facing, place the blue spotted shoe piece on top of the white, or blue, felt piece and sew the shoe together along the centre fronts and along the upper shoe edge. Trim the seams neatly, snipping into the corners and curves, then turn the shoe to the right side and press.

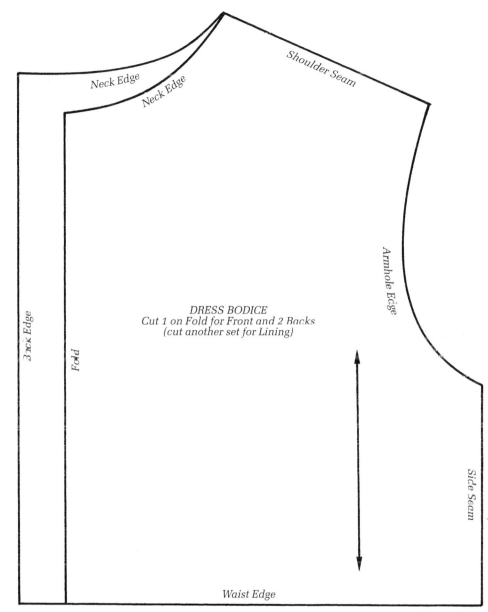

DRESS BODICE
*Cut 1 on Fold for Front and 2 Backs
(cut another set for Lining)*

Neck Edge · Neck Edge · Shoulder Seam · Armhole Edge · Back Edge · Fold · Side Seam · Waist Edge

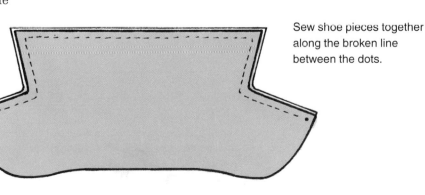

Sew shoe pieces together along the broken line between the dots.

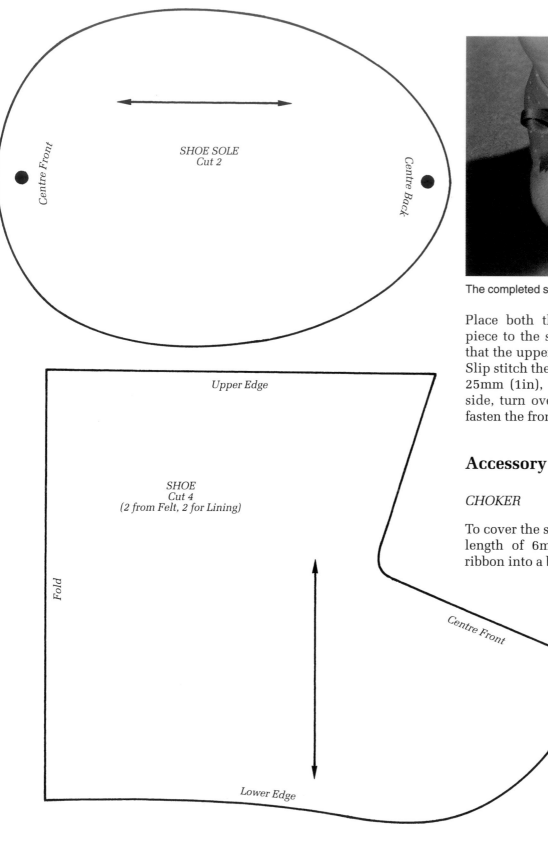

The completed shoe.

Place both thicknesses of lower shoe piece to the sole and sew into place so that the upper shoe is joined to the sole. Slip stitch the centre front of the shoe for 25mm (1in), turn the shoe to the right side, turn over the top of the shoe and fasten the front with a blue satin bow.

Accessory

CHOKER

To cover the sewing at the neckline, tie a length of 6mm (¼in) wide blue satin ribbon into a bow.

SHOE SOLE
Cut 2

Centre Front

Centre Back

Upper Edge

SHOE
Cut 4
(2 from Felt, 2 for Lining)

Fold

Centre Front

Lower Edge

5 The Topsy-Turvy Rag Doll

THE BASIC TOPSY-TURVY RAG DOLL

The topsy-turvy rag doll is a double-headed doll, and is a great favourite with children. It may also be referred to as a happy/sad doll since, quite often in the past when these dolls were made, they would have been given a happy face at one end and a sad face at the other with a solitary tear upon one cheek. They can also be made so that they have different coloured hair: one fair, and the other dark. Furthermore, some were made using different fabric colours for the faces, showing half of the doll to be black and the other half to be white. The dolls featured in this book have been created to allow a child to play out the character of the stories upon which they are based.

All of the doll faces are embroidered, which means that you can give your doll any expression you wish: the topsy-turvy dolls shown here have been given expressions to suit their characters. For instance, the Cinderella doll shows a sad face in her Cinders outfit, but by slightly altering the mouth to make her smile, she appears happy in her ballgown; the Sleeping Beauty doll, as a result of pricking her finger on the spinning-wheel, has been given a sleeping face, and a happy face for when she is awoken by the prince.

The Prince Charming doll shown in the book can be made to accompany either Cinderella or Sleeping Beauty by altering the colours and style in which he is dressed.

The outfits for the topsy-turvy doll can be made to fit the medium-sized rag doll, provided they are made singly. It is therefore possible to make Cinderella or Sleeping Beauty as ordinary dolls, to accompany Prince Charming.

MATERIALS

- a piece of cream-coloured cotton fabric measuring 915mm × 458mm (36 × 18in)

- a quantity of stuffing

- a selection of embroidery silks for the doll's face

- tracing paper

Making the Doll

Trace all of the relevant pattern pieces from the book onto tracing paper, making sure that you transfer all of the markings to your pattern pieces. Place all the pattern pieces onto the cream-coloured cotton fabric, ensuring that the arrows indicated on the pattern line up with the selvedge of the material. Before separating the pattern pieces from the fabric, transfer any markings that might be required. Then cut out two topsy-turvy doll pieces from the material and, with a well-sharpened pencil,

Tracing features on the same side of the doll.

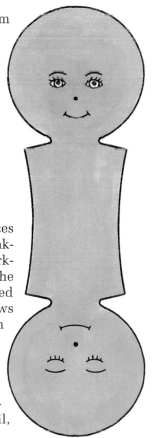

93

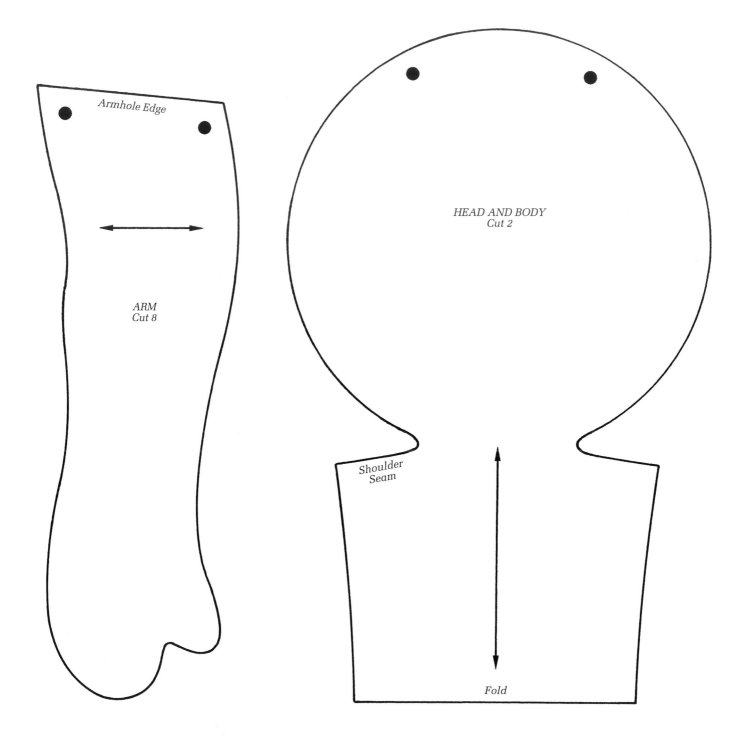

trace the face features onto the right side of one of these pieces.

With right sides facing, sew the body pieces together, allowing a 6mm (¼in) seam all around the doll and taking care to leave an opening at the top of both of the doll's heads between the

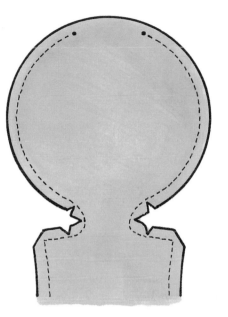

(*far left*) Sew along the broken line between the dots.

(*left*) Snip notches around the curved edges.

heads will permit the doll to be stuffed more easily.

Fill the body and heads completely with stuffing until the doll feels firm, then finish off by sewing up the opening on both of the heads with a neat ladder stitch.

Cut out two pairs of arm pieces from the fabric and, with right sides together, sew around each pair between the dots. Trim the seams neatly and snip into the curved edges at the thumb to allow the material to sit properly. Turn the pieces to the right sides and stuff the arms firmly to within 13mm (½in) of armhole edge. In order to prevent the raw edge of the material from fraying, turn over and sew a 6mm (¼in) hem, then gather up the stitches tightly and sew each arm securely in position at the shoulder seam, as indicated on the pattern. The doll is now finished.

Sew arm pieces together as shown by the broken lines.

dots, so that the assembled doll can be turned to the right side later. Trim the seams neatly and snip away excess fabric from the curved edges, enabling the material to sit properly. Leaving the opening at the top of each of the doll's

THE CINDERELLA RAG DOLL

The Cinderella rag doll allows a child to play out the fairy tale without having to dress and undress the doll. One way around, Cinderella appears in her Cinders outfit; by turning the skirt the other way, she appears in all her glory to attend the ball.

MATERIALS

◆ basic topsy-turvy rag doll

◆ a 500 × 915mm (19¾in × 36in) piece of lilac satin fabric

◆ a 500 × 915mm (19¾in × 36in) piece of lilac cotton fabric

◆ a 305 × 458mm (12 × 18in) piece of pink flowered cotton fabric

◆ 1m (39⅜in) of white lace 90mm (3½in) wide

◆ 500mm (19¾in) of white lace 38mm (1½in) wide

- ◆ 750mm (29½in) of dull-coloured lace 19mm (¾in) wide

- ◆ 500mm (19¾in) of white lace 13mm (½in) wide

- ◆ 750mm (29¼in) of lilac satin ribbon 13mm (½in) wide

- ◆ 250mm (9¾in) of lilac narrow satin ribbon 3mm (⅛in) wide

- ◆ 1m (39⅜in) of silver rickrack braid

- ◆ 50g of yellow double knitting yarn

- ◆ an assortment of coloured embroidery silks

- ◆ oddments of coloured fabric for patches

- ◆ a short length of thin elastic

- ◆ small scraps of iron-on interfacing

- ◆ fourteen lilac satin roses

- ◆ one lilac satin bow with pearls

- ◆ velcro or pop fasteners

Features

Before sewing the topsy-turvy rag doll together, transfer both of Cinderella's features onto the two heads (as shown for the Bride Doll on page 46), making the mouth for the Cinders doll less happy. The choice of silks for the embroidering of the features should take account of the hair colour: the illustrated doll being fair suggests that the silks should be of more natural shades. Both faces are embroidered with identical coloured silks. The colour chosen for the outline of the eyes, eyebrows and

(*right*) Decoration of hair.

nose is a light caramel, the mouth is a soft dusky pink and the eyes a beautiful cobalt blue.

Hair

HAPPY DOLL

The hair for the doll attending the ball has been made quite elaborate. For the back of the hair, cut a template 75mm (3in) wide by 100mm (4in) long, wind yellow double knitting yarn around it fifty times, sew the yarn along both edges, slip it from the template and sew to the seam at the side of the head, in line with the features. Sew a line of stitches down the back of the yarn to form a parting. To make the side of the hair, cut a card template 100mm (4in) wide by 125mm (5in) long, wind the yarn around it forty times, sew along one edge of the template, and then slip the yarn very carefully from the template, using a matching piece of yarn to tie it into a bunch at the unsewn end. Place the sewn edge of the yarn down the back of the head from the centre top, and secure the bunches to the side of the head with a few stitches. Make an identical piece for the other side of the head. To make the bun at the back of the head, use the same template as for the side hair, but this time wind the yarn around it twelve times. Taking two pieces of the same yarn, tie the hair at each end of the template, then carefully ease the yarn from the template. Make a loose knot to secure the ends, place the bun to the back of the head and sew into place. To make the fringe, which consists of a cluster of loops, form each cluster by winding the yellow yarn around the index and middle fingers ten times, ease them off and tie in the centre with a matching piece of yarn, fastening the cluster to the front of the head by sewing

the tie in the middle of the loop with a few stitches. Three clusters should be sufficient for the whole of the fringe. Decorate the hair by sewing three lilac satin roses to the top of the bun and a lilac satin bow with pearls to its centre, and wind a piece of 3mm (⅛in) lilac narrow satin ribbon around each bunch of loops at the side of the head.

CINDERS DOLL

Cut a card template 100mm (4in) wide by 203mm (8in) long, wind the yellow yarn around 100 times, sew the yarn together along one end of the template, cut it at the other end and then open the yarn out flat and use the line of sewing as a centre parting down the back of the head. Secure the line of sewing at the front of the head and stitch into place down the centre back. Divide each side into three equal amounts and form a plait down the side of the head, tie them with a piece of matching yarn, and decorate the plaits by knotting an old scrap of fabric around the ends. To make the fringe, cut a card template measuring 50mm (2in) wide by 50mm (2in) long, wind the yarn around the template approximately twenty times, sew the yarn together along one edge and snip it at the other. Stitch the sewn edge of the hair along the centre front of the seam. Any gap at the back of the head will be hidden under the mob cap, but if you wish to cover the back of the head completely, use the instructions given for the spiral method elsewhere in the book.

Note that the length of each template refers to how long you wish the hair to be.

Skirts

Cut out two skirt pieces from your chosen fabrics, each measuring 235 × 702mm (9¼ × 30in). Placing the right sides of the fabric together along the long edges, sew the skirt pieces together taking a 6mm (¼in) seam which will form the skirts' hemline. Open up the skirt pieces, place them with right sides facing, and sew between the dots marked on the pattern, which will now create the back seam of the skirts. Turn the skirts to

the right sides and decorate both pieces before joining them onto the bodices. The dresses in the book are made from the same colour but a different fabric: one is made from a lilac cotton and the other from a lilac satin.

The ballroom skirt is made from the lilac satin and is decorated elaborately. Sew a piece of 90mm (3½in) wide white lace along the skirt, matching up the scalloped edge of the lace with the hemline. Sew a 762mm (30in) length of silver rickrack along the top of the lace, and decorate the lace with lilac satin roses – or an alternative decoration such as bows.

The Cinders skirt is made from the lilac cotton fabric, and is decorated much more plainly with a 19mm (¾in) wide dull-coloured lace sewn 63mm (2½in) above the hemline. You will then need to cut out a few different coloured patches which need to be backed with iron-on interfacing to stop them from fraying too much; sew each of the patches onto the skirt using big stitches in a contrasting colour.

With the wrong sides of the skirts facing, turn a 6mm (¼in) hem to neaten the raw edges along the back opening, slip stitch the opening together and run a gathering stitch along the waist edge through both fabrics to join the skirt pieces together.

Ballroom Bodice

Cut out one bodice front and two bodice backs from the lilac satin fabric, as shown on the pattern. With the right sides together, take a 6mm (¼in) seam and sew the front and back bodice pieces together along the side and shoulder seams, trimming neatly. From a piece of lilac cotton fabric, cut out and sew another bodice in the same way to be used as a lining. With right sides

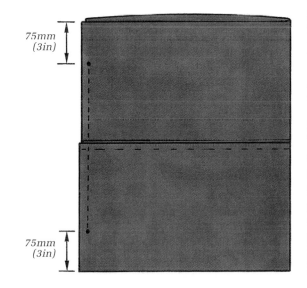

75mm
(3in)

75mm
(3in)

(*left*) Sew along the broken line between the dots to form the back seam of the skirts.

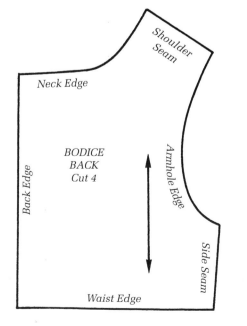

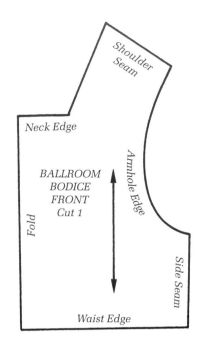

BALLROOM
BODICE
FRONT
Cut 1

Shoulder Seam

Neck Edge

Fold

Armhole Edge

Side Seam

Waist Edge

together, sew the bodice pieces to the lining at the back edges and along the neckline. Trim the seams and snip into corners and curves, turn the bodice to the right side and press. Using a tacking stitch, sew the bodice and lining together at the armhole and waist edges.

SLEEVES

Cut out two sleeve pieces from the lilac satin fabric as shown on the pattern. With right sides of fabric facing, take a 6mm (¼in) seam and sew the underarm seam, and then turn a double 6mm (¼in) hem along the lower sleeve edge to form a casing for the elastic. Sew a length of 38mm (1½in) wide white lace to the upper edges of the casing, thread elastic through the casing and secure it to the required length. Gather the upper sleeve between the dots, ease the sleeve into the bodice, matching up the sleeve seam to the armhole bodice seam, and sew it into place. Trim the armhole edges neatly and oversew the raw edges.

BODICE
BACK
Cut 4

Shoulder Seam

Neck Edge

Back Edge

Armhole Edge

Side Seam

Waist Edge

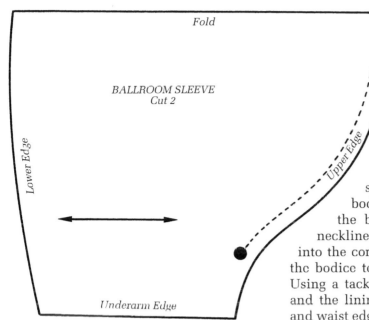

sides together, take a 6mm (¼in) seam and sew the front and back bodice pieces together along the side and shoulder seams, trimming the seams neatly. Cut out and sew another bodice in the same way to be used as a lining. With right sides together, sew the bodice pieces to the lining at the back edges and along the neckline. Trim the seams and snip into the corners and curves, then turn the bodice to the right side and press. Using a tacking stitch, sew the bodice and the lining together at the armhole and waist edges.

Cinders Bodice

Cut out one bodice front and two bodice back pieces from the lilac-coloured cotton fabric, as shown on the pattern. With right

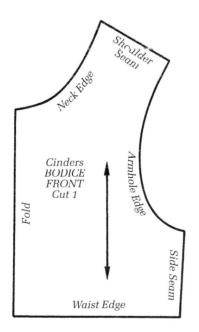

SLEEVES

Cut out two sleeve pieces from the lilac cotton fabric, as shown on the pattern, turn a double 6mm (¼in) hem along the lower edge of the sleeve and, with the right sides of the fabric together, join the underarm edges taking a 6mm (¼in) seam. Make a tuck at the top of the sleeve to allow it to fit into the armhole of the bodice, then sew the sleeve into place, over-sewing the raw edges. Make a line of contrasting stitches along the bodice to represent a tear which has been repaired.

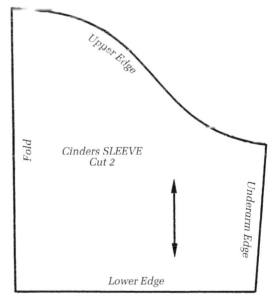

Matching Bodices to Skirts

Gather the waist edge of the skirts and sew a 6mm (¼in) seam, joining the right sides of the bodices along the waist edge to the corresponding skirt, thus creating a sandwich effect. Trim the seams neatly and oversew the raw edges. Finish off the bodices by sewing velcro or pop fasteners along the back opening to enable the bodices to be fastened shut.

To finish the dresses, decorate the bodice of the ballgown by sewing a 50mm (2in) length of 13mm (½in) wide white lace across the centre front of the bodice and gather up the front of the lace with a few stitches. Using the same white lace, sew another piece into place along the back neck edge, over the shoulder seam and down the front of the bodice to the waist. Turn the lace to form a V at the waistline and sew it into position up the other side of the bodice, over the shoulder to the centre back. Take a 500mm (19¾in) length of 13mm (½in) wide lilac satin ribbon, place it around the waist, securing it with a bow at the back of the dress. Make a lace rosette by using a 100mm (4in) length of 13mm (½in) wide white lace, sew a line of gathering stitches along the straight edge of the lace and pull the stitches together to form a circle. Sew the narrow raw edges of the lace together and decorate the centre of the rosette with a lilac satin rose, sewing it to the centre front of the bodice over the lilac satin ribbon.

Use a small length of silver rickrack to form a necklace, cut to fit around the neck and sewn with a few firm stitches.

Mob Cap

Cut a 178mm (7in) diameter circle from a piece of pink flowered cotton fabric, turn a double 6mm (¼in) hem around the outside of the circle to neaten, sew a line of gathering stitches around the mob cap 32mm (1¼in) from the outer edge and pull the gathering stitches to fit the head. Sew the mob cap into place at the centre front and back of the Cinders doll's head.

Apron

Cut out two pieces from the remaining pink flowered cotton fabric, one measuring 125mm (5in) long by 150mm (6in) wide to be used as the apron skirt, and another measuring 305mm (12in) long by 32mm (1¼in) wide to be used as ties. Take a 6mm (¼in) hem around the edges of the apron, leaving one 150mm (6in) side unsewn. Gather the unsewn edge until it measures 63mm (2½in) wide and then, with the right sides of the fabric facing, sew the apron skirt to the centre of the apron ties. Folding the tie of the apron so that the right sides are together, take a 6mm (¼in) seam and sew around the tie, leaving an opening to correspond with the apron skirt.

Turn the ties to the right side and press. Finally, turn under a 6mm (1/4in) hem and slip stitch the ties to the apron skirt, encasing the seam.

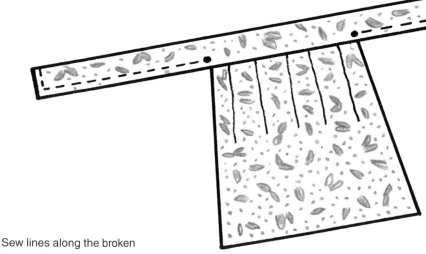

Sew lines along the broken line as shown.

THE SLEEPING BEAUTY RAG DOLL

The story of Sleeping Beauty has been told in many ways. Our rag doll is shown pricking her finger and falling into a deep sleep wearing her day dress; and then, when the prince awakens her from her sleep, she transforms into a birthday ballgown for the happy ending.

MATERIALS

- ◆ basic topsy turvy doll

- ◆ a 330 × 915mm (13 × 36in) piece of pink shantung silk fabric

- ◆ a 355 × 915mm (14 × 36in) piece of white and pink flowered cotton fabric

- ◆ 100 × 230mm (4 × 9in) of white cotton fabric

- ◆ 1m (39⅜in) of white lace with scalloped design 38mm (1½in)wide

- ◆ 500mm (19¾in) of white lace 25mm (1in) wide

- ◆ 500mm (19¾in) of white lace 6mm (¼in wide)

- ◆ 500mm (19¾in) of pink satin ribbon 16mm (⅝in) wide

- ◆ 500mm (19¾in) of green and gold ribbon 25mm (1in) wide

- ◆ 1.5m (59in) of green narrow satin ribbon 3mm (⅛in) wide

- ◆ 50g of yellow double knitting yarn

♦ an assortment of embroidery silks

♦ 1m (39¾in) of gold braiding 25mm (1in) wide

♦ gold lurex thread

♦ one gold pipe cleaner

♦ one gold ribbon rose

♦ velcro or pop fasteners

Features

Before sewing the topsy-turvy rag doll together, transfer both of Sleeping Beauty's features onto the two heads. (awake features as for the Bride Doll on page 46, asleep features as shown here). For the choice of embroidery silks, note that the doll has fair hair, and therefore the silks should be of the more natural shades. The face of the sleeping doll is embroidered using a pale dusky pink for the mouth and a light caramel colour for the eyelids, eyebrows and nose; the colours for the happy face are the same, and a cobalt blue for the eyes.

Sleeping Beauty's features.

Hair

ASLEEP DOLL

Using a card template measuring 100mm (4in) wide by 230mm (9in) long, wind the yellow double knitting yarn around it 100 times, and sew along one edge, securing the yarn so that it measures approximately 32mm (1¼in) across. Snip it at the opposite end of the template. Taking the sewn edge of the hair, sew it to the head at the centre front where indicated at the

dots. To make plaits, cut six pieces of yarn 458mm (18in) long, secure the strands together at one end with a knot, then divide the yarn into three sections of two strands each and plait them, knotting the remaining hair together. Fasten one end at the nape of the neck, looping it around the loose hair, and secure this end of the plait alongside the first end at the nape. Take the centre of the plait and sew this to the centre of the head, approximately 50mm (2in) from the front. Now, to keep the hair in place when the doll is turned upside down, make another six-stranded plait, this time only 230mm (9in) long. Sew it to one side of the head along the seam line, level with the mouth, loop it around the back of the hair and sew it into place in the corresponding position on the other side of the head.

Cut a piece of green and gold ribbon measuring 230mm (9in) long, find the centre of the ribbon and place the raw edges to overhang the centre. Tack along the centre to join the ribbon, pulling the tacking stitches to form it into a bow. Decorate the centre of the bow by winding the gold lurex thread around it. Sew the completed bow to the back of the head at the top of the plait.

To make the fringe, once again use the yellow double knitting yarn and wind it around two of your fingers twelve times, secure the loops together and sew them into place at the dot indicated at the front of the head.

AWAKENED DOLL

Cut a card template measuring 100mm (4in) wide by 230mm (9in) long, and wind the yellow double knitting yarn around it 100 times, sewing along one edge of the template so that the yarn, measures about 32mm (1¼in) across. Snip the yarn at the opposite end of the template. Taking the sewn edge of the hair, sew it to the head as indicated by the dots. To make the plaits, use approximately thirty-six strands of the yarn from the front of the head and divide them into three equal parts, plait the hair and secure the plaits to the back of the head with a few stitches 100mm (4in) from the front of the hairline.

For the fringe, repeat the procedure for the asleep doll of winding yarn around two fingers twelve times, securing together and sewing into place at the dot shown at the front of the head.

To decorate the hair, make a pink satin bow. Cut two pieces of pink satin ribbon, one measuring 150mm (6in) long, the other 305mm (12in) long. Join the 150mm (6in) piece together by overlapping the raw edges, fold the 305mm (12in) piece in half and sew it to the back of the first piece over the raw

Sew plaits to the side of the head, securing the back of the hair in place.

edges. Wind the 305mm (12in) ribbon around the other, securing them together with a gold rose in the centre, and leave the remaining ends loose. Sew into place over the join where the plaits meet at the back of the head.

Decorating the back of the hair.

Skirts

Cut out two skirt pieces from your chosen fabrics, each measuring 235 × 762mm (9¼ × 30in). Placing the right sides of the fabrics together along the long edges, take a 6mm (¼in) seam to form the skirt's hemline and sew the skirt pieces together. Open up the skirt pieces and, placing them with right sides facing, sew a 6mm (¼in) seam along the back edges between the dots to form the back seam of the skirts. Turn the skirts to the right sides and decorate along both hemlines before joining them onto the bodice. The dresses in the book are made to show a contrast. The dress for when Sleeping Beauty is asleep after she has pricked her finger is decorated with a 38mm (1½in) wide white lace sewn 25mm (1in) above the hemline of the skirt; make and sew a small green and gold bow along the scalloped edge of the lace all the way around. The party dress after she has awakened to the prince's kiss is decorated with just a single row of 25mm (1in) wide gold braiding sewn along the hemline. With the wrong sides of the skirts facing together, turn a 6mm (¼in) hem to neaten the raw edges along the back opening, and slip stitch the opening together. Run a gathering stitch along the waist edge through both fabrics, joining the skirt pieces together.

Sew along the broken line between the dots to form the back seam of the skirts.

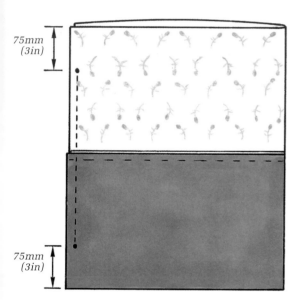

75mm (3in)

75mm (3in)

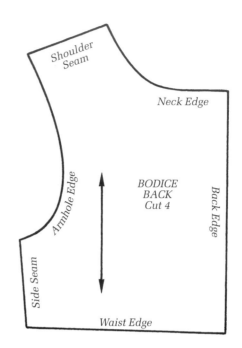

as shown on the pattern. With right sides together, take a 6mm (¼in) seam and sew the front and back bodice pieces together along the side and shoulder seams, trimming them neatly. Cut out and sew another bodice in the same way, this time using white cotton fabric, to be used

Flowered Bodice

To make the flowered bodice, cut out one bodice front and two bodice back pieces

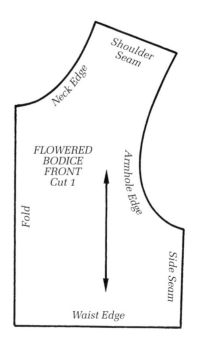

as a lining. With right sides of fabric together, sew the bodice pieces to the lining at the back edges and along the neckline. Trim the seams and snip into the corners and curves. Turn the bodice to the right side and press. Using a tacking stitch, sew the bodice and the lining together at the armhole and waist edges.

SLEEVES

Cut out two sleeve pieces as shown on the pattern. Turn a 6mm (¼in) hem along the sleeve's lower edge, sew a 25mm (1in) wide lace trimming along the hemline of each sleeve, and, with the right sides of the fabric together, join the underarm edges, taking a 6mm (¼in) seam. Gather along the upper edge of each sleeve between the dots as shown on the pattern, matching the sleeve seams to the side seams of the bodice. Ease the top of the sleeve to fit into the bodice armhole, then sew it into place. Trim the seams neatly and oversew the raw edges. Along the lower edge of the sleeve, sew together the two dots which

will form a small pleat; make and sew a green satin bow to finish off the sleeve.

Sew a satin bow to decorate the pleat in the sleeve

Party Bodice

To make the pink shantung bodice, cut out one bodice front and two bodice backs as shown on the pattern. With right sides together, take a 6mm (¼in) seam and sew the front and back bodice pieces together along the side and shoulder seams, trimming neatly. Cut out and sew another bodice in the same way to be used as a lining. With the right sides of the fabric together, sew the bodice pieces to the lining at the back edge and along the neckline. Trim the seams and clip into the corners and curves. Turn the bodice to the right side and press. Using a tacking stitch, sew the bodice and the lining together at the armhole and waist edges.

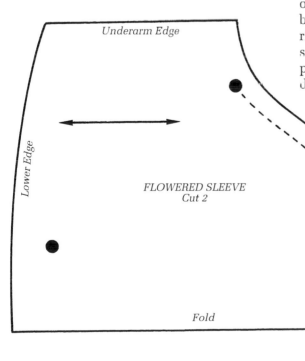

Underarm Edge

Lower Edge

FLOWERED SLEEVE
Cut 2

Upper Edge

Fold

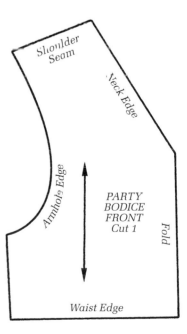

Shoulder Seam

Neck Edge

Armhole Edge

PARTY BODICE FRONT
Cut 1

Fold

Waist Edge

SLEEVES

Cut out two sleeve pieces as shown on the pattern, turn a 6mm (¼in) hem along the lower edge of the sleeve and sew a length of gold lurex thread along the sleeve edge to cover the line of sewing. With right sides together, join the underarm edges taking a 6mm (¼in) seam. Gather along the upper edge of each sleeve between the dots, as shown on the pattern, matching the sleeve seams to the side seams of the bodice, then gather the top of the sleeve to fit into the bodice armhole, sewing the sleeve into place. Trim the seams neatly and oversew the raw edges.

Lower Edge

Underarm Edge

PARTY SLEEVE
Cut 2

Fold

Upper Edge

Matching Bodices to Skirts

Gather the waist edge of the skirt and, with the right sides together, sew it to the lower edges of the bodices, taking a 6mm (¼in) seam. Trim the seams neatly and oversew the raw edges. To finish off the dresses, the bodices will need to be decorated. For the flowered dress, gather a piece of narrow white lace, approximately 203mm (8in) long, and sew it to the inside of the neckline. Make a green satin bow and sew it into place at the centre front of the bodice. The illustrated doll has a wide sash of green and gold ribbon caught at the front with gold lurex thread. The raw edges of the sash are turned over and secured to the back of the bodice.

The party dress has a trimming of gold lurex thread sewn around the neckline, and a piece of gold braiding – which is identical to the braiding sewn along the skirt hemline – is used to decorate the waist. Secure the braiding along the waistline and sew firmly to the back of the dress.

Finally, so that the bodice can be fastened shut, sew velcro or pop fasteners along the back opening.

Sew lines along the broken line as shown.

Crown

To make the crown, you will need a gold-coloured pipe cleaner. You may bend this into any design you wish; it is then sewn into place at the top of the head.

6 The Child-Sized Rag Doll

THE BASIC CHILD-SIZE RAG DOLL

The child-sized rag doll is a bigger version of the large rag-doll, in as much as it represents the size of a child approximately two years of age. The sewing techniques are identical to those used in the making of the large rag doll, but, in addition, she has been given lines of sewing on each hand to give the appearance of fingers.

MATERIALS

◆ a piece of cream-coloured cotton fabric measuring 915 × 915mm (36 × 36in) from which all the pattern pieces are cut

◆ a large quantity of stuffing

◆ heavy-duty card

◆ a selection of different-coloured embroidery silks for the doll's face

◆ tracing paper

Making the Doll

Trace all the relevant pattern pieces from the book onto tracing paper, making sure that you transfer all markings where indicated. Some of the patterns in the book have had to be split up in order to fit them onto a page. The pattern

pieces will show exactly where they should be joined together by the letters A and B.

Place all of the pattern pieces onto the cotton material, making sure that you line up the arrows shown on the pattern piece to the selvedge of the material.

Before removing all of the pattern pieces from the material, mark any darts which may be required, as well as the dots such as those that show where the head gusset joins the head front and back pieces. Place the cut-out front head piece on top of the doll's face and trace the features onto the fabric with a well-sharpened pencil.

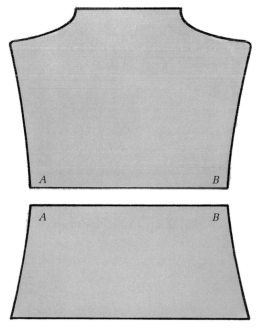

Join the pattern pieces A and B.

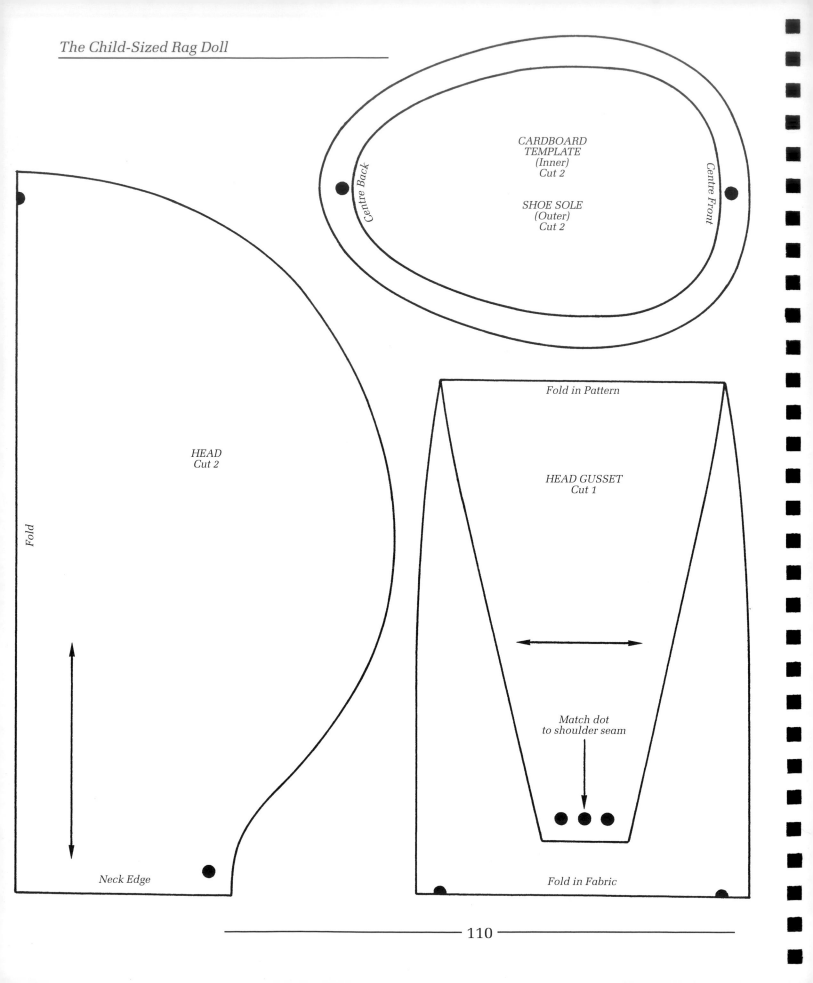

CARDBOARD
TEMPLATE
(Inner)
Cut 2

Centre Back

Centre Front

SHOE SOLE
(Outer)
Cut 2

HEAD
Cut 2

Fold

Neck Edge

Fold in Pattern

HEAD GUSSET
Cut 1

Match dot
to shoulder seam

Fold in Fabric

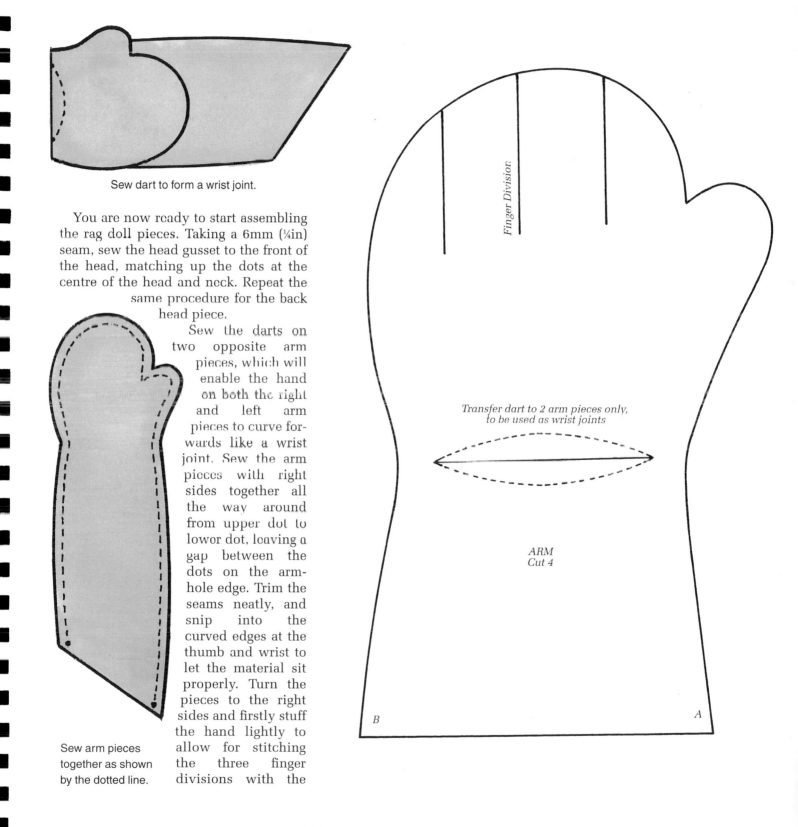

Sew dart to form a wrist joint.

You are now ready to start assembling the rag doll pieces. Taking a 6mm (¼in) seam, sew the head gusset to the front of the head, matching up the dots at the centre of the head and neck. Repeat the same procedure for the back head piece.

Sew the darts on two opposite arm pieces, which will enable the hand on both the right and left arm pieces to curve forwards like a wrist joint. Sew the arm pieces with right sides together all the way around from upper dot to lower dot, leaving a gap between the dots on the armhole edge. Trim the seams neatly, and snip into the curved edges at the thumb and wrist to let the material sit properly. Turn the pieces to the right sides and firstly stuff the hand lightly to allow for stitching the three finger divisions with the

Sew arm pieces together as shown by the dotted line.

Finger Division

Transfer dart to 2 arm pieces only, to be used as wrist joints

ARM
Cut 4

B

A

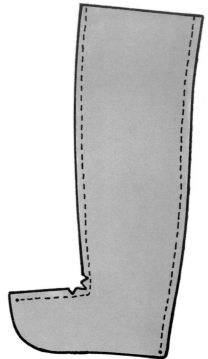

Stitch between the dotted lines to close the armhole edge.

(*right*) Cut notches at ankle curve.

sewing machine. If the hand is over-stuffed at this stage, it will not fit under the machine. These finger divisions are clearly shown on the main pattern. Now continue stuffing the arm firmly to within 32mm (1¼in) of the armhole edge, and close the seam with a tacking stitch.

Taking a 6mm (¼in) seam, join the centre front and centre back seams of the leg pieces. Trim the seam neatly, and snip into the front seam at the ankle curve. Matching the dot on the sole piece to the front and back seams of the

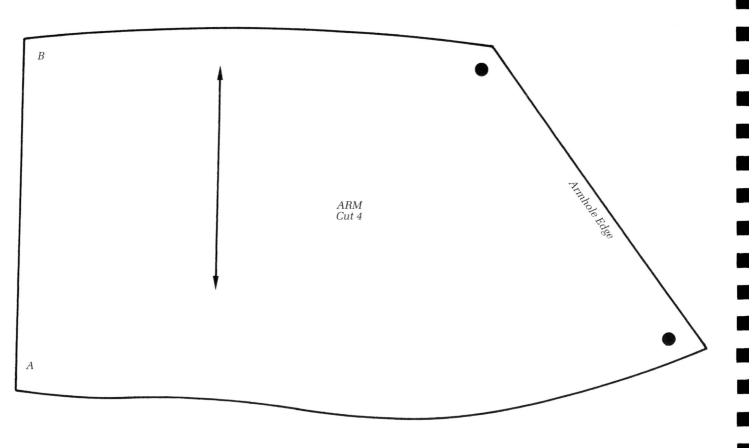

B

ARM
Cut 4

Armhole Edge

A

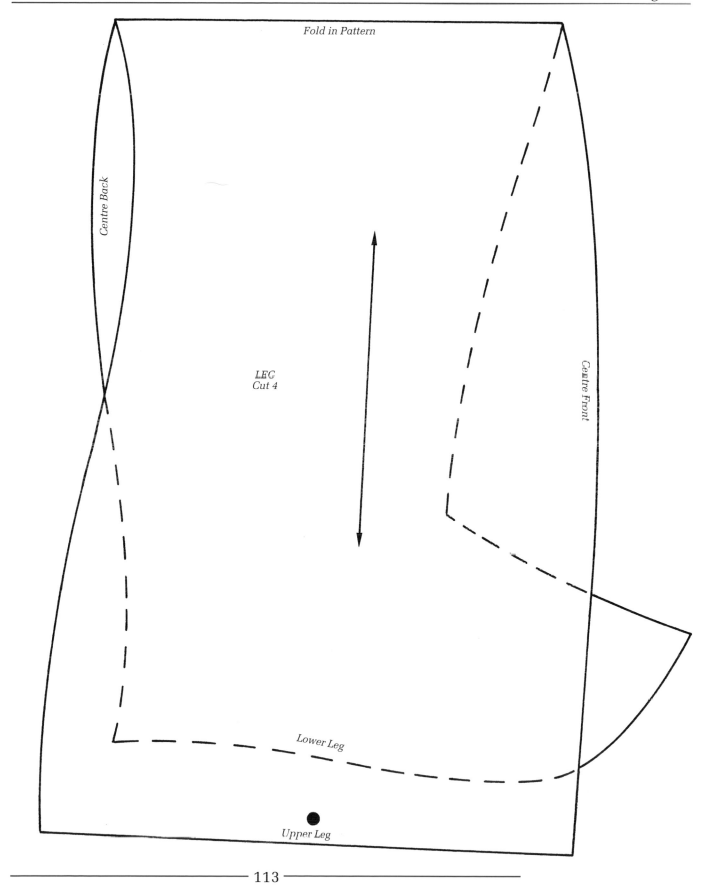

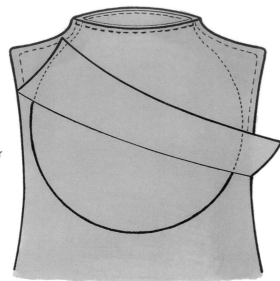

Matching the dots on the head gusset to the shoulder seams, sew the body onto the head.

Sew the shoulder seams on the body pattern. This will now leave a hole into which the head is sewn. Matching the dots on the head gusset to the shoulder seams, sew the body onto the head. Tack the arms to the right side of the body pieces between the dots, making certain that the arms are facing inwards. Sew both legs at the bottom of the body pattern, matching the dots, and ensuring that the legs are both facing the right way.

leg pieces, sew a 6mm (¼in) seam around the base of the foot, joining the leg to the sole. Trim the seam neatly, and turn the leg to the right side. Cut a sole piece out of heavy-duty card, making sure that you follow the inside pattern piece from the book, and place inside the finished foot. Stuff the leg firmly to within 32mm (1¼in) of the upper leg, closing this with a tacking stitch.

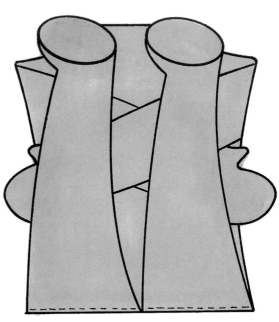

Join the legs to the body piece, making sure they are the right way round.

Sew the body pieces right sides together up the side seams, placing the arms crossed over inside the body pieces. Turn the doll to the right side, and begin to stuff the head, making sure that the neck is as firm as possible. Continue stuffing the remainder of the body until you are satisfied with the finished result. Sew the bottom of the body pieces together using a ladder stitch. The doll is now complete and ready to be dressed.

Join the arms to the body piece, making sure that they are facing the right way round.

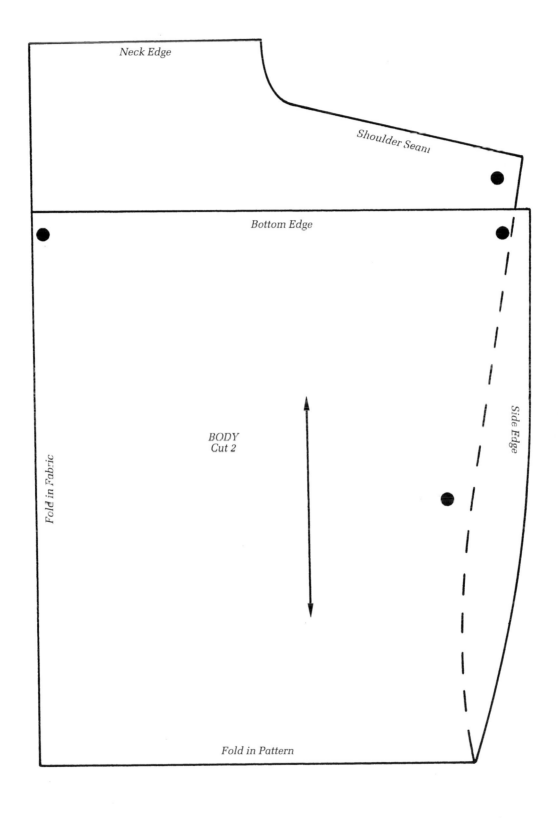

Neck Edge

Shoulder Seam

Bottom Edge

Side Edge

Fold in Fabric

BODY
Cut 2

Fold in Pattern

THE SNOW CHILD
RAG DOLL

This rag doll will probably appeal to adults more than to children, as it pictures exactly how a Victorian girl would be dressed on a snowy winter's day.

MATERIALS

- ◆ basic child-sized rag doll

- ◆ a 1.5m × 915mm (59 × 36in) piece of burgundy velvet fabric

- ◆ a 1,000 × 915mm (39⅜ × 36in) piece of black flowered cotton fabric

- ◆ a 750 × 1,525mm (29¼ × 60in) piece of burgundy polyester viscose fabric

- ◆ a 750 × 1,144mm (29¼ × 45in) piece of cream flowered cotton fabric

- ◆ a 500 × 915mm (19¾ × 36in) piece of cream cotton fabric

- ◆ 4m (157½in) of cream fur fabric 50mm (2in) wide

- ◆ 2.25m (88½in) of cream broderie anglaise lace 50mm (2in) wide

- ◆ 3m (118in) of cream gathered broderie anglaise lace 25mm (1in) wide

- ◆ 3m (118in) of cream lace 13mm (½in) wide

- ◆ 500mm (19¾in) of cream lace 6mm (¼in) wide

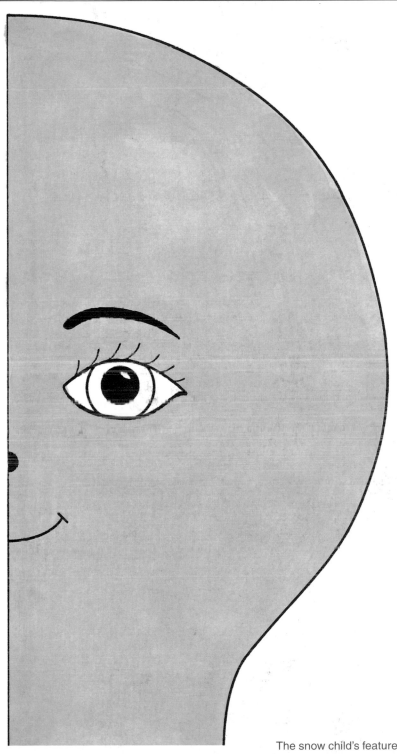

- ◆ 1m (39⅜in) of cream satin ribbon 25mm (1in) wide

- ◆ 2.75m (108¼in) of black flowered ribbon 6mm (¼in) wide

- ◆ 150g of dark brown double knitting yarn

- ◆ an assortment of coloured embroiders silks

- ◆ a 305 × 458mm (12 × 18in) piece of black felt or velvet

- ◆ 500mm (19⅝in) of elastic 6mm (¼in) wide

- ◆ four black flowered buttons

- ◆ four gold-coloured buttons

- ◆ four gold-coloured beads

- ◆ velcro or pop fasteners

Features

Before sewing the rag doll together, transfer the snow child's features onto the front of the head. When selecting the colours of the silks, consider that the doll is dark, so it is best to embroider the eyebrows and eye outline in dark brown to complement the hair, whereas the nose should be a shade lighter, with the eyes a dark blue and the mouth a rich red.

Hair

To make a fringe, cut a card template 203mm (8in) wide by 90mm (3½in) long, and wind the yarn around the template approximately eighty times. Sew the yarn together securely along one edge of the card and snip it at the other. Take the

The snow child's features.

sewn edge of the hair and sew it into place along the front seam of the head. Now make a second template, this time measuring 280mm (11in) wide by

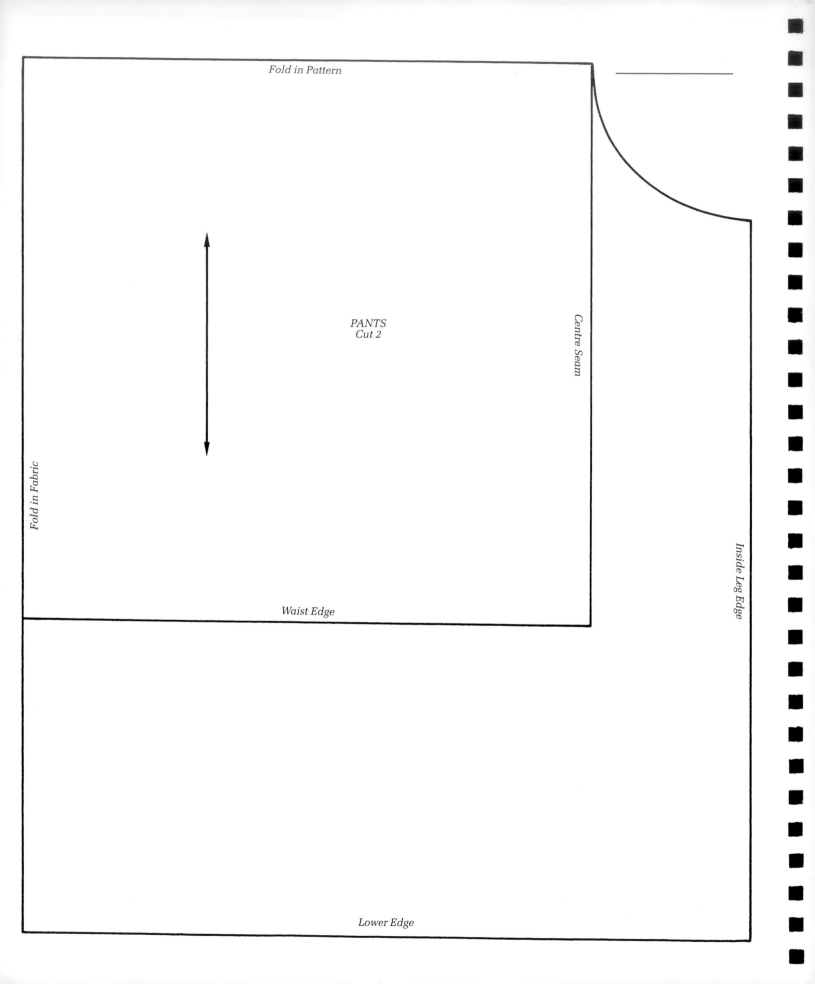

Fold in Pattern

PANTS
Cut 2

Fold in Fabric

Centre Seam

Inside Leg Edge

Waist Edge

Lower Edge

330mm (13in) long, and wind the yarn around it 150 times. Sew the yarn firmly together along one edge, as previously, and cut it at the other. Place the sewn edge of the hair to the back of the doll's head 100mm (4in) down from the centre top of the head.

For the remaining hair, cut a third template, measuring 203mm (8in) wide by 406mm (16in) long, and wind the yarn around it 150 times, sewing and snipping as before. Take the sewn edge of the hair and sew it into place at the front seam of the head just behind the fringe. Trim the hair at the back of doll until the hair is all one length. To decorate, cut a piece of 25mm (1in) wide cream satin ribbon, measuring 356mm (14in) long, tie the ribbon into a bow and stitch it into place along the top of the head.

The length of each of the three card templates denotes how long you wish the hair to be.

Pants

Cut out two pants pieces from the cream cotton fabric. Turn and sew a double 6mm (¼in) hem along the lower edge of the pants pieces. Decorate the hemline with a row of 13mm (½in) wide cream lace, and sew another row 25mm (1in) above the first. With the right sides of the fabric together, sew a 6mm (¼in) seam to join the

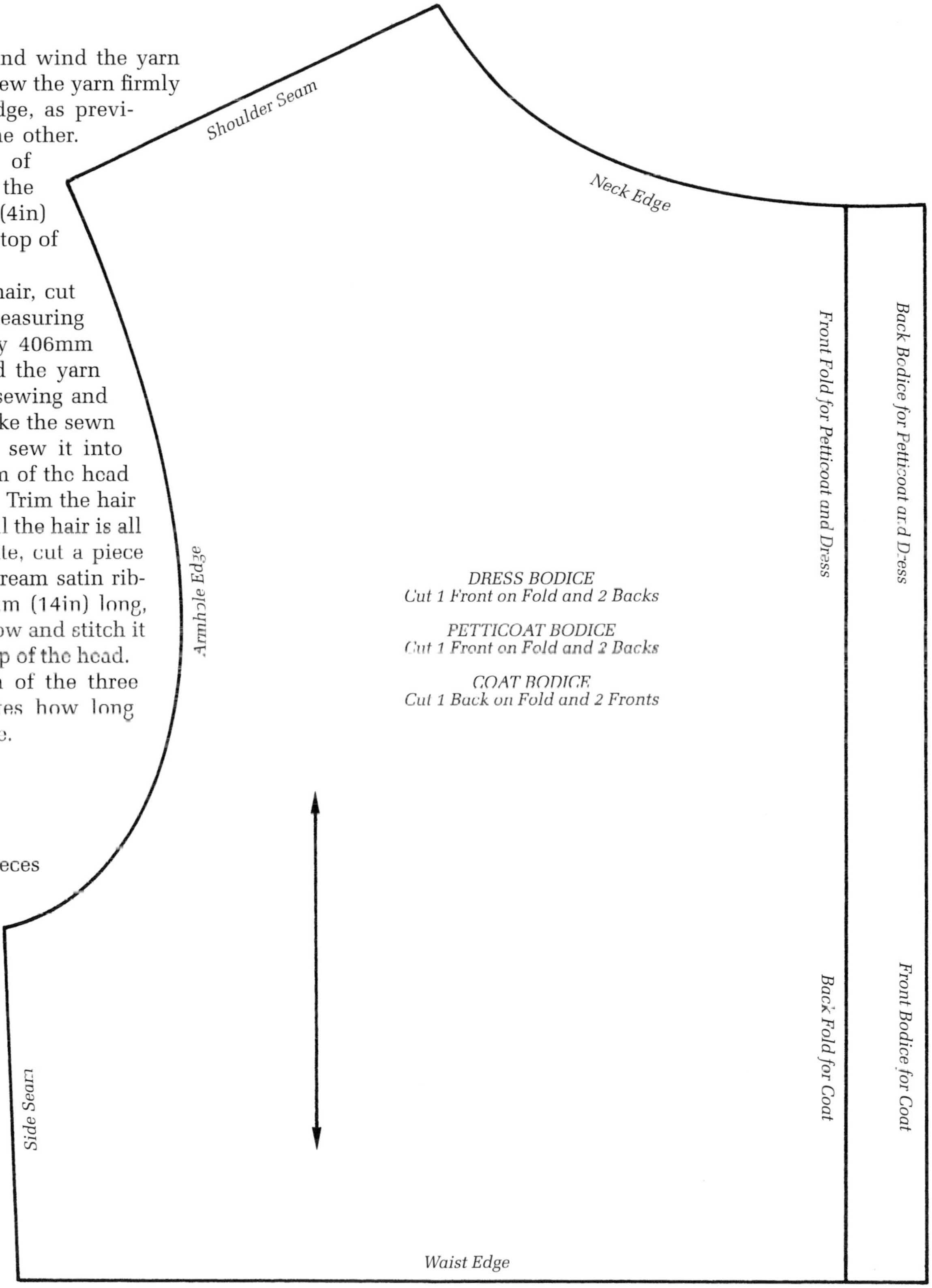

Shoulder Seam

Neck Edge

Armhole Edge

Side Seam

Front Fold for Petticoat and Dress

Back Bodice for Petticoat and Dress

Back Fold for Coat

Front Bodice for Coat

DRESS BODICE
Cut 1 Front on Fold and 2 Backs

PETTICOAT BODICE
Cut 1 Front on Fold and 2 Backs

COAT BODICE
Cut 1 Back on Fold and 2 Fronts

Waist Edge

inside leg edges, and do the same for the other pants piece. Join the pants pieces together, taking a 6mm (¼in) seam along the centre seams. Trim the seams neatly and snip into the curves. Turn a double 6mm (¼in) hem along the waist edge to form a casing for the elastic, then thread the elastic through the casing and fasten it to the required length.

Petticoat

From the cream flowered cotton fabric, cut out one bodice front and two bodice backs. With the right sides of the fabric facing, take a 6mm (¼in) and sew the front and back bodice pieces together along the side and shoulder seams. Trim the seams neatly. Cut out and sew another bodice in either the cream flowered cotton fabric or just a plain cream cotton fabric to be used as lining. Taking the bodice and lining, place them with right sides together and sew a 6mm (¼in) seam along back and neck edges. Trim the seams and snip into the corners and curves. Turn the bodice to the right side and press. Turn in a 6mm (¼in) hem along the armhole edges on both the bodice and lining and slip stitch together. Sew a length of 13mm (½in) wide cream-coloured lace on the front of the bodice 50mm (2in) below the neckline.

To make the petticoat skirt, cut a piece of cream flowered cotton fabric 1,144mm (45in) wide by 356mm (14in) long, and mark the fabric into quarters along the waist edge. Turn a double 13mm (½in) hem along the

The completed petticoat.

lower edge of the petticoat. For decoration, sew a 1,144mm (45in) length of 13mm (½in) wide cream lace 75mm (3in) above the hemline. With the right sides of the fabric facing, take a 13mm (½in) seam along the back edge of the petticoat, leaving a 75mm (3in) opening at the waist edge. Sew a double 6mm (¼in) hem at the back opening to neaten it. Gather the waist edge of the petticoat skirt and match up the quarter division marks on the skirt with the appropriate bodice markings, such as the bodice back, side seams and centre front. Taking a 6mm (¼in) seam, sew the petticoat skirt and bodice together, making sure to leave the bodice lining free. Turn under a 6mm (¼in) hem at the waist edge of the bodice lining and slip stitch the lining to the waist seam to finish off. For further decoration, make and sew a pink satin bow to the centre front, and sew a length of 6mm (¼in) wide cream-coloured lace along the waist seam. Secure the back opening with either velcro or pop fasteners.

Dress

Cut out two bodice fronts and four bodice backs from the burgundy polyester viscose fabric, one set to be used as a lining. With the right sides of the bodice pieces together, take a 6mm (¼in) seam and sew the front and back pieces together along the side and shoulder seams. Trim the seams neatly, and then repeat the same procedure to make the lining. With the right sides of the bodice and lining facing, join them together at the back edge and along the neckline. Trim the seams and clip into the corners and curves. Turn the bodice to the right side and press.

Cut out two sleeve pieces from the burgundy polyester viscose fabric, turn a double 13mm (½in) hem along the lower

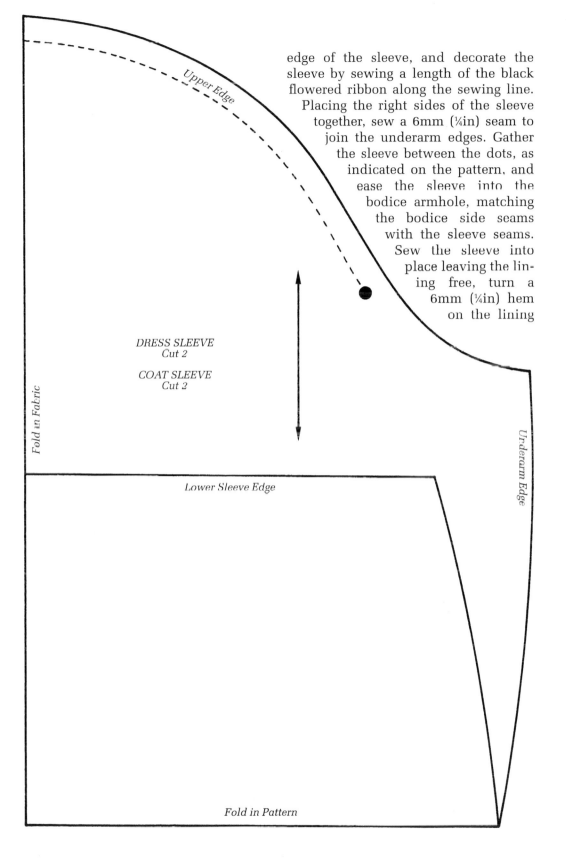

Upper Edge

DRESS SLEEVE
Cut 2

COAT SLEEVE
Cut 2

Fold in Fabric

Underarm Edge

Lower Sleeve Edge

Fold in Pattern

edge of the sleeve, and decorate the sleeve by sewing a length of the black flowered ribbon along the sewing line. Placing the right sides of the sleeve together, sew a 6mm (¼in) seam to join the underarm edges. Gather the sleeve between the dots, as indicated on the pattern, and ease the sleeve into the bodice armhole, matching the bodice side seams with the sleeve seams. Sew the sleeve into place leaving the lining free, turn a 6mm (¼in) hem on the lining

The completed dress.

(*right*) Sew along the broken line between the dots and snip into curves.

armhole and slip into place, encasing the armhole raw edges. Decorate the neck edge of the bodice by sewing a length of 25mm (1in) wide gathered broderie anglaise along the neckline.

To make the skirt, cut a piece of burgundy polyester viscose fabric, measuring 1,525mm (60in) wide by 406mm (16in) long, and mark the fabric into quarters to line up with the bodice later. Turn a double 25mm (1in) hem along the lower edge of the skirt. To decorate, sew a 1,525mm (60in) length of 50mm (2in) wide cream broderie anglaise along the hemline, placing the top of the broderie anglaise 75mm (3in) above the edge of the hem, and then sew a length of black flowered ribbon along the top of the broderie anglaise to cover the sewing line. Placing right sides of the skirt together, sew a 13mm (½in) seam along the centre back edges, leaving a 75mm (3in) opening at the waist edges. Turn a double 6mm (¼in) hem to neaten the back opening. Gather the waist edge of the skirt, matching up the quarter divisions made on the skirt with the appropriate bodice markings, such as the bodice back, side seams and centre front. Taking a 6mm (¼in) seam, sew the skirt and bodice pieces together, making certain to leave the lining free. Turn under a 6mm (¼in) hem along the waist edge of the bodice lining, and slip stitch the lining along the waist edge to

encase the raw edges. Decorate the waistline by sewing a length of 50mm (2in) wide cream broderie anglaise around the bodice at the waist, matching up the scalloped edge of the broderie anglaise with the waist seam. To neaten the top of the broderie anglaise, cover the raw edges with a length of 6mm (¼in) wide black flowered ribbon and sew into place. Fasten the back edges of the bodice with velcro or pop fasteners.

Coat

From the burgundy velvet, cut out one bodice back and two bodice fronts. With the right sides of the fabric facing, take a 6mm (¼in) seam and sew the front and back bodice pieces together along the side and shoulder seams. Trim the seams neatly. Cut out and sew another bodice from the black flowered cotton fabric to be used as a lining. Cut out two collar pieces, one from the burgundy velvet and the other from the black flowered cotton fabric. With the right sides of the fabric facing, join the collar pieces together, taking a 6mm (¼in) seam and leaving open the neck edge seam to allow the collar to be turned to the right side. Trim the seams neatly and snip into the curves. Turn the collar to the right side and press. Line up the neck edge of the collar along the neck-

line of the bodice and place the bodice lining on top of the collar, forming a sandwich. Taking a 6mm (¼in) seam, sew the bodice together along the back and neck edge. Trim the seams and snip into the corners and curves. Turn the bodice to the right side and press.

Cut out two sleeve pieces from the burgundy velvet, turn a double 6mm (¼in) hem along the lower edge of the sleeve and, placing the right sides of the sleeve together, sew a 6mm (¼in) seam to join the underarm edges. Gather the sleeve between the dots and ease it into the bodice armhole, matching the bodice side seams with the sleeve seams. Sew into place, leaving the lining free, turn a 6mm (¼in) hem on the lining armhole and slip stitch into place, encasing the sleeve and armhole raw edges.

To make the skirt of the coat, cut a piece of burgundy velvet measuring 1,626mm (64in) by 432mm (17in) long (or two pieces each measuring 813mm (32in wide by 432mm (17in) long which will need to be joined together at the back), and mark the fabric into quarters to line up with the bodice later. Turn a double 25mm (1in) hem along the lower edge of the skirt, then turn a double 13mm (½in) hem along the short edges of the skirt which will form the front opening. To decorate, sew a length of fur fabric 50mm (2in) wide around the hemline of the skirt. Gather the waist edge of the skirt matching up the quarter divisions made on the skirt with the appropriate bodice markings, such as the centre back, side seams and centre front opening. Taking a 6mm (¼in) seam, sew the skirt and bodice pieces together, making sure to leave the lining free. Turn under a

6mm (¼in) hem along the waist edge of the bodice lining, and slip stitch the lining along the waist edge to encase the raw edges. Decorate the coat by sewing four black flowered buttons along the bodice front. To enable the coat to be fastened, sew a strip of velcro, or position some pop fasteners, to the centre front of the bodice.

Hood and Cape

Cut out one hood and one cape pattern from the burgundy velvet fabric. With right sides of the fabric facing, take a 6mm (¼in) seam along the centre back of the hood and, placing the fabric together, join the hood and the cape at the neck edge. Cut out and sew another hood and

Fold

COLLAR
Cut 2
(1 as Lining)

Neck Edge

Centre Back

Centre Back

Fold in Pattern

HOOD
Cut 4
(2 as Lining)

Neck Edge

Outer Edge

cape from the black flowered cotton fabric to be used as a lining. Join the hood and the cape to the lining by placing the right sides of the fabric together and sewing a 6mm (¼in) seam around the outer edges, leaving a 150mm (6in) opening at the back of the cape to enable you to turn the

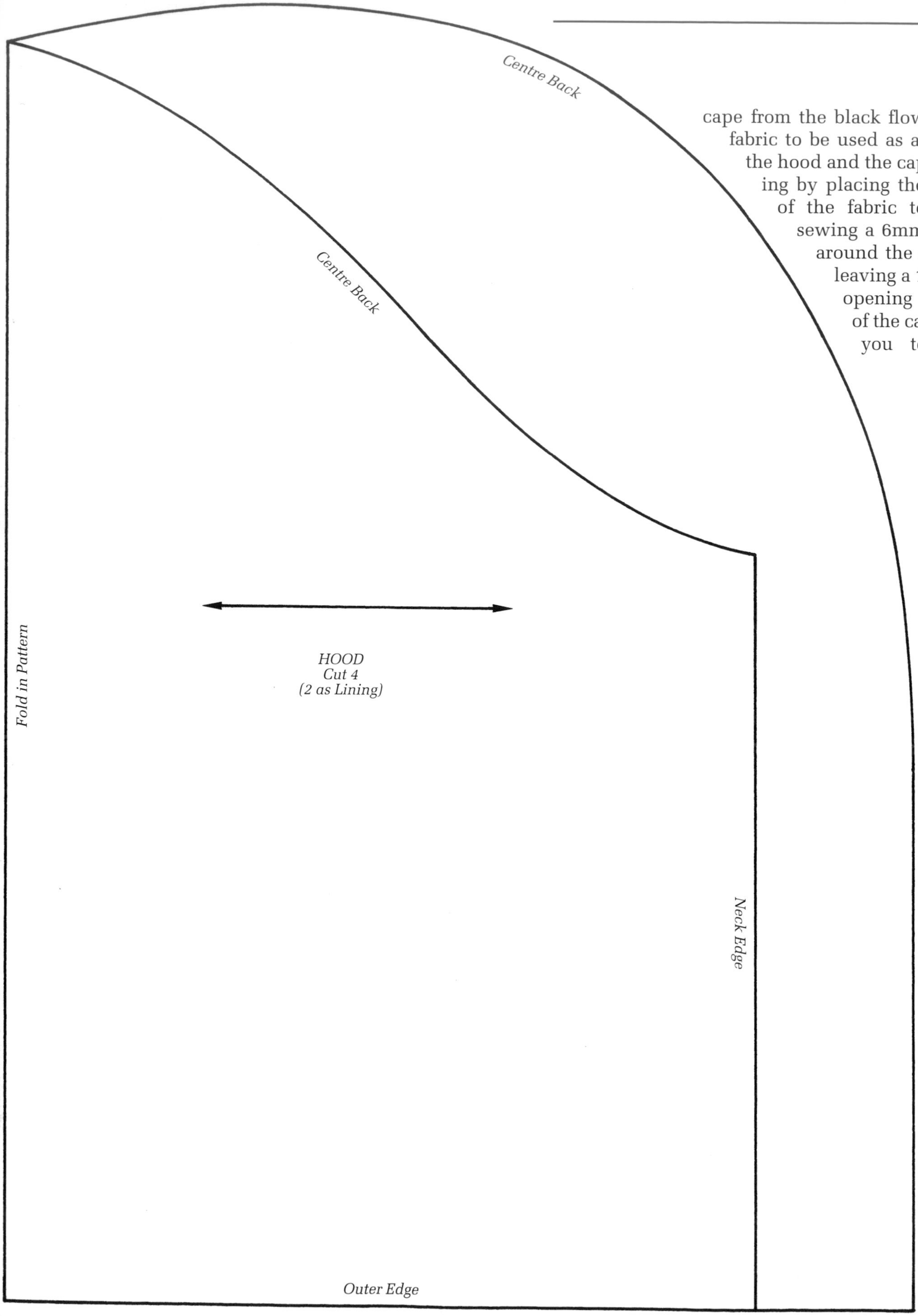

CAPE
*Cut out 2 Full Capes,
1 as Lining*

Neck Edge

Fold

Outer Edge

Fold (×8, radiating lines)

garment to the right side. Trim the seams neatly and snip into any corners and curves. Turn the garment to the right side and press. Slip stitch the 150mm (6in) opening at the base of the cape. Trim all outer edges with a strip of fur fabric 50mm (2in) wide. To permit the cape to be fastened, cut two lengths of cream satin ribbon measuring 356mm (14in) long by 25mm (1in) wide. Sew the ribbon to the two neck edges of the cape, which can now be tied into a bow.

Shoes

Cut out two shoe pieces and two shoe soles from the black felt or velvet; also cut out two shoe pieces from the black flowered cotton fabric. Altogether, this will make both shoes. With the right sides of the fabric together, place the black flowered shoe piece on top of the black felt or velvet piece and sew the shoe together along the centre fronts and the upper shoe edge. Trim the seams and snip into the corners and curves, then turn the shoe to the right side and press. Place both thicknesses of the lower shoe piece to the sole and sew into place so that the upper shoe is joined to the sole. Slip stitch the centre front of the shoe for 100mm (4in), turn the shoe to the right side, fold over the top of the shoe and sew two gold-coloured buttons along the centre front, attaching a small gold-coloured bead to the folded piece of shoe as decoration.

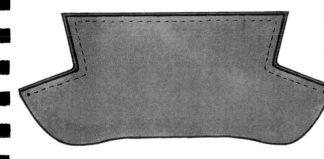

Sew the shoe pieces together along the broken line between the dots.

The completed shoes

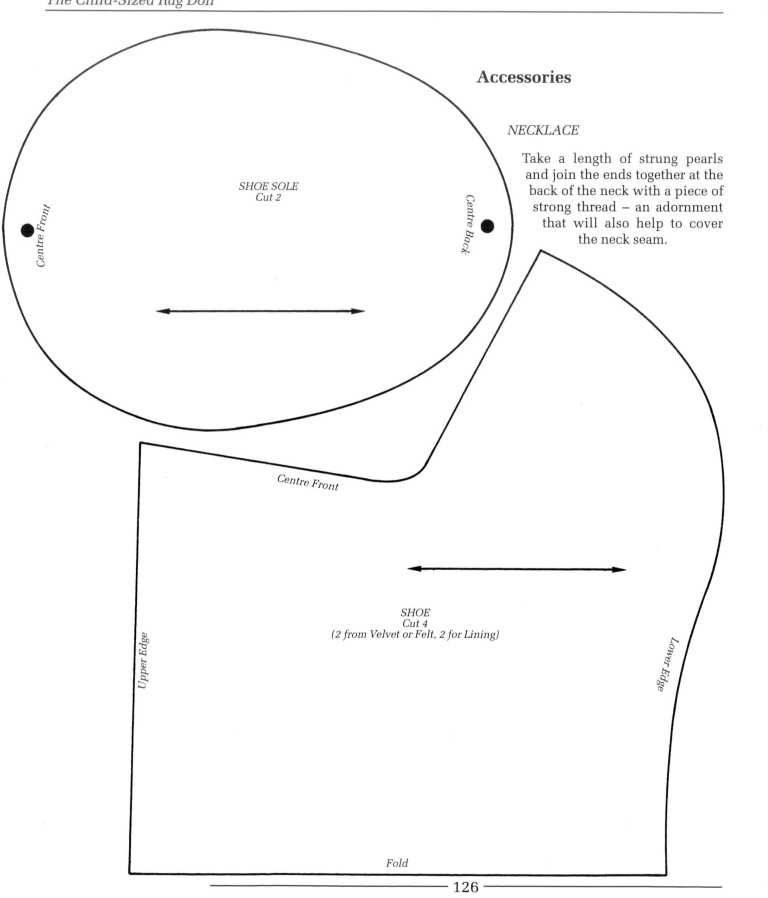

Accessories

NECKLACE

Take a length of strung pearls and join the ends together at the back of the neck with a piece of strong thread – an adornment that will also help to cover the neck seam.

SHOE SOLE
Cut 2

Centre Front

Centre Back

Centre Front

Upper Edge

Lower Edge

SHOE
Cut 4
(2 from Velvet or Felt, 2 for Lining)

Fold

Index